How to become
RICH &
SUCCESSFUL

CHARLES TEMPLETON

How to become
RICH &
SUCCESSFUL

*A 14-Point
Plan for Business Success*

PIATKUS

This edition first published in
Great Britain in 1990 by
Judy Piatkus (Publishers) Ltd of
5 Windmill Street, London W1P 1HF

First published in Canada
in 1989 as "Succeeding"

The excerpt from "Two Tramps in Mud Time" on p. 52 of this book is reprinted from *The Poetry of Robert Frost*, Edward Connery Lathem ed. Copyright 1936 by Robert Frost and renewed 1964 by Lesley Frost Ballantine. Used by permission of Henry Holt and Company, Inc., New York.

British Library Cataloguing in Publication Data
Templeton, Charles
  How to become rich and successful.
  1. Business enterprise. Success
  I. Title
  650.1

  ISBN 0-7499-1012-7

Printed and bound in Great Britain by
Mackays of Chatham PLC, Chatham, Kent

For my father
William Loftus Templeton
who unwittingly convinced me
that I could achieve
anything I wanted to

A FABLE

LONG AGO in a small village there lived a very wise man. There was a boy in the town who didn't like the wise man and decided to trick him. He caught a small bird, and cupping it in his hands so that only its tail feathers could be seen, took it to the wise man.

"Is this bird alive or is it dead?" he asked.

If the wise man said it was alive the boy planned to give it a quick squeeze and open his hands to show the bird was dead. If the wise man said the bird was dead, he would open his hands and let it fly away. So no matter what the wise man said, he would have him.

"Is it alive or is it dead?" the boy asked.

The wise man looked, not at the boy's hands but into his eyes and said, "It's whatever *you* want it to be."

Contents

Introduction

THIS BOOK is based on three premises:

- That success is not reserved for the extraordinarily gifted; it is available to anyone who will seek it with commitment and imagination.
- That most men and women are working nowhere near their potential, usually because they don't know how to take advantage of the opportunities around them.
- That advancement in business does not result from hard work alone but from the commitment of the mind.

You will not find in these pages a list of simplistic techniques, the exercising of which will make certain your advancement and wealth. Nor will you find a litany of psychological mantras guaranteed to raise your self-esteem and unleash your potential.

Succeeding is never that simple.

This book will tell you that, if you set your mind to it, you can enhance your abilities, multiply your opportunities and increase your income. And it will show you how to transform your work from a daily drudgery to an exciting experience.

The subject of this book is not success in life but success in business. The second does not necessarily lead to the first but for most the second is fundamental to the first.

If you are a failure at work the fallout is liable to contaminate everything else in your life and contribute not only to your own unhappiness but to the unhappiness of those close to you. Find satisfaction and a sense of achievement in work and you are more likely to enjoy the other areas of life: family, home, friends, intellectual pursuits, the arts, leisure, play.

It is probable that in your lifetime you will work eight-hour days, five days a week, fifty weeks of the year for fifty years. In each of these 13,000 days you will sleep eight hours, work eight hours and have eight hours for your leisure. Which means that *one half of your waking life is spent at work*. What a monumental mistake not to use that time well, not to take full advantage of the opportunity to realize your potential and thus to win the financial rewards and the satisfaction that work well done can bring.

Self-imposed limitations

Here is the tale of two working men.

The first man spends a year going client to client selling a product and ends the year having earned twenty thousand dollars. The other spends the year organizing and directing a sales campaign that will earn his company twenty million dollars. Each puts in the same number of hours but the first ends the year worrying about his loan at the bank while the other is promoted to a senior job and given a bonus equal to the first man's earnings.

It is not that one worked harder than the other, but that the first man worked mindlessly. He was industrious. He was conscientious. He met his quotas. He satisfied his superiors, and he will be secure in his job for the remainder of his life.

But he merely put in time.

The other man used time. Over the year he committed not just his hands but also his mind to the job. He viewed his work not as an obligation but as an opportunity. He realized that the potential for success was in him and he concentrated on developing it. He appraised his abilities and focused on improving what he did well. He observed that there is very little difference between the merely competent and the very successful and determined to make up the difference. When he encountered problems he didn't curse them but worked to solve them. He looked for needs and sought to meet them. He noticed that most of what happens in any office depends on communicating — by the written or the spoken word — and set out to acquire the requisite skills. He discovered that the most valuable ability in business is the capacity to make the right decisions most of the time, so he studied the decision-making process. It dawned on him that there is a better way to do *anything*, and he never forgot it.

He worked to make himself needed and ended up making himself indispensable.

The first man did not remain mired in his job for want of trying — if by trying is meant the set jaw, the furrowed brow and the willingness to work hard — he failed to succeed because he accepted the limitations on the job he had been given to do.

A similar inertia afflicts most men and women. They do not look beyond the task at hand. Some because they don't know how to apply the abilities they have and others because, while they feel the stirrings of ambition, they have only vague notions as to how to go about improving those abilities.

It is not a lack of resolve, it is more a lack of imagination. They are confused as to what steps to take. As a consequence, they are often angry at themselves or at others or at "the system," and are frustrated because they don't quite know how to get off the mark.

This book will attempt to speak to such problems.

The sense of achievement

Only you know what you want from life. Only you know how far your horizons reach. Only you know what your goals are.

Or do you?

Millions don't. They do little introspection. They make few long-term plans. They hope simply to "muddle through." If they do succeed it is more often than not the result of favorable connections or pure luck. But the odds against that happening are about the same as winning the lottery.

This book is not written for such. It is written for men and women who have given thought to what they want from life and are prepared to pay the price to get it. And that's the point: There is a price to be paid. To assert otherwise, to suggest that success is a prize to be won without imagination and with little effort would be to mislead.

This book will set before you some techniques for success. They have been learned in almost fifty years of experience in a wide variety of fields. Although his formal education ended at grade nine, they have enabled the author to progress from menial jobs to positions of authority in great corporations. They have enabled him to speak from public platforms to tens of thousands in a dozen countries. They have opened the doors to television as an executive, a producer, a writer and a performer. They have equipped him to direct complex activities, to counsel others, to hire and fire, to meet payrolls and to perform effectively under the pressures of running a great metropolitan newspaper. They have also produced the self-reliance needed to concentrate during long periods of isolation in the writing of ten books.

Beyond that, they have made work an adventure.

Winning satisfaction

As you begin, let this be clearly understood: None of the ideas put forward in this book are presented as infallible solutions to the multiple and diverse problems of the workplace.

They call for commitment. They will not work for the nine-to-fiver. They are offered in the conviction that, while success in the workplace is not achieved easily, it and its rewards are available to anyone who will seek them. You may not stand the world on end — each of us has different gifts — but as the author, Thomas Wolfe, expressed it: "If a man has a talent and learns somehow to use the whole of it, he has gloriously succeeded, and won a satisfaction and a triumph few men ever know."

1 | The Winning Edge

THERE IS A PRINCIPLE at the heart of life: Life is not what you find, it is what you create.

You are born with two things: existence and opportunity, and these are the raw materials out of which you can make a successful life.

Most men and women want to find happiness, but you don't *find* happiness any more than you *find* steel. You refine steel from the rough ore and you fashion happiness from life's opportunities.

The artist doesn't *find* a beautiful statue; he sculpts it from the shapeless marble.

The musician doesn't find an intricate melody; she composes it from the eight-note scale.

And so it is with you. You are given an intellect; you can use it or let it stagnate. You are given a body; you can keep it fit or let it deteriorate. You are given 365 days in the year; you can use them or waste them.

At work you are given an opportunity: you can turn it into an adventure or let it descend into drudgery.

You can succeed or you can fail. The choice is yours.

Success is no secret

The one thing you can't do is succeed without effort.

"But," you ask, "are there people who believe they can succeed in business without really trying?"

You bet! The world is full of men and women who do little more than meet their basic obligations.

They are the nine-to-fivers, the timeservers, people who never miss a coffee break, who arrive on the stroke of nine and have their desks clear five minutes before quitting time.

They are decent people, most of them, pleasant, interesting, up on the latest movies, never too busy to talk about last night's ball game or the latest trend in fashions or the current office scuttlebut.

They do their job. They meet their obligations. They take the initiative in organizing and raising money for the office party. They move ahead in the company as their turn comes. And when the time arrives for them to retire, everyone has a kind word for "Good old John," or for "That marvelous girl, Mary."

But they never take work home. They never come up with a new idea. They never raise questions. They never seek to improve accepted procedures. They never initiate change.

But if they are satisfied with their jobs and if they earn their paychecks, whose business is it but theirs? Not everyone has to be a world-beater.

Let it be understood: not everyone has a need to be president of the company or the top sales person or the creative whiz. And no criticism is implied. But let this also be understood: these are the people who make it easy for anyone who really wants to succeed in business to do so.

Success in business is no secret. Unless you are the boss's child, success is a matter of *wanting* to succeed, wanting to enough to put in extra hours, to concentrate fully, to challenge your mind and your imagination.

It comes down to commitment.

Not to repeat the foolish cliché that "anyone can be president"; of course not. We are not all equally gifted. But if you want success badly enough and are prepared to work hard for it, there is every reason to believe you can achieve it.

The prerequisite is to believe that you can.

Not simply by setting your jaw and resolving to. Not by repeating some psychological incantation about releasing the untapped potential within you. Not by attending seminars or reading books. Success derives from a combination of three things: rigorous thought, hard work and maximizing your abilities.

The winning edge

You may think back at this point, "I'm not going to delude myself. There are men and women in the company better equipped for success than I am. They are better educated, more personable and more driven than I am. How can I hope to surpass them?"

Begin by refusing to erect inappropriate standards. Don't measure yourself against hypothetical rivals; you are evaluating *your* potential, not theirs. And in the world of business, the difference between winners and losers actually is very small.

Have you not had the experience of meeting (or seeing on television) some extraordinary achiever, someone of whom you may have been in awe, and being surprised at how downright "ordinary" he or she seemed to be?

The fact is, the difference between the celebrated and the also-rans is small. Occasionally, successful people have had more than the average number of breaks, but more often, success has come because they have fixed their minds on it and worked hard to achieve it.

Compare the averages of the great and the run-of-the-mill hitters in major-league baseball. The difference between the great hitter and the journeyman is surprisingly small.

George Brett isn't twice as good as that player who was shipped to the minors in mid-season; he is merely better. In a given year, a Brett might hit .330 and a Joe Mediocre .230. A big difference? It seems so, but reduced to its essentials what is that difference? When Brett comes to bat, the odds are that he will get a hit *one time in three.* When our journeyman steps to the plate, the odds are that he will get a hit *one time in four.*

Get a hit once in three at-bats and you are an All-star major leaguer. Get a hit once in four and you are in danger of being shipped to the boondocks.

That relatively small difference—one extra hit in ten times at bat—is the reason we hail the Joe DiMaggios and the Ted Williamses and forget most of the others.

Most of the great baseball players live and eat and sleep the game. There are exceptions: sports geniuses like Babe Ruth and Mickey Mantle, who broke all the rules — but they are just that: exceptions. The difference between most of the stars and most of the others does not lie in their intellects or their muscular prowess—but in the fact that they are willing to pay the price required to boost them to success.

What is that price? Hard work, steely dedication and exceptional commitment.

It is such things as extra time at batting practice each day, a carefully considered change in stance at the plate, total concentration on the opposing pitcher's motion while in the dugout awaiting a turn at bat, frequent discussions with the coaches, working out daily, maintaining physical conditioning in the off season.

A lot of little things.

Daily things.

The winning edge is small

The difference between success and mediocrity in business is not very different. The salesperson who makes eighty thousand dollars a year is not twice as good as the person who makes forty thousand. The first one works a little harder, concentrates a little more, plans a little more carefully, knows the job a little better, refines skills with greater care and is ready to make that extra effort.

Line up a dozen salesmen and ask which are the successful, which are average and which are the failures. A casual observer will be unable to tell. The difference is in the inner man.

It is in his attitude. In his dedication. In his concentration. In his commitment to his work.

Trace the history of a class graduating from a major business school. Although these men and women attended the same classes, received the same training and fulfilled the same assignments, their subsequent achievements range all the way from outstanding success to dismal failure.

Nor will their successes and failures necessarily reflect their class standings.

There will be graduates who came to maturity more slowly than others, who didn't "find themselves" until later than is usual.

There will be straight-A's who bomb in the business world for any number of reasons.

There will be others who, out from under the disciplines of regimented study, can't get themselves motivated.

And there will be, of course, many who perform as might have been predicted.

But beyond all these there will be another group.

They may have done poorly in the classroom. They may have gotten caught up in extracurricular activities and neglected to hit the books. They may have barely scraped through their senior year, graduating without distinction. But they have been eminently successful in the world of business.

More often than not the reversal has come about because, after graduation, they took a hard look at themselves and made a conscious act of commitment.

The improvement in their performance may not have been more than twenty percent, but that twenty percent is the winning edge.

Preparedness makes for competence

How can you go about improving your performance? Approach it as you would any other challenge.

If you made the decision to improve your physical condition, you would undertake a program of exercise. You would work out daily, seeking to improve your strength, your endurance and your vascular fitness. Within a few months your energy level would be higher and you would feel a new zest for life.

If a regimen of physical self-improvement can so improve your body, do you doubt that a similar program to improve your mind would work equally well?

"But," you say, "the development of physical fitness is a science. We know that muscles systematically flexed become stronger and that cardiovascular capacity can be increased. But is this true of the mind?"

Why not the mind? Don't scholars increase their ability to think through study? The brain is subject to the same laws that govern the body: neglect it and it atrophies, challenge it and it develops.

If you work on your command of English for a year do you doubt that you would become more knowledgeable, better able to communicate your thoughts, more comprehending of what you read?

If you spend the next twelve months learning everything you can about the business you are in, wouldn't your performance improve, your confidence increase and your ability be sharpened?

Greater opportunities in business may depend upon your merely doing better what you do now.

There are few better opportunities to impress your worth on your colleagues and your boss than in the staff meetings that are frequent occurrences in every business. The atmosphere is casual. There may be no chairman; everyone regarding the others as their peers.

But because these are informal meetings, there is a temptation to approach them with the intention of winging it: waiting until the direction of the meeting has been established and then trusting your inventiveness. This is a major mistake.

You may be quick with responses, capable of reacting with cogent comments or spur-of-the-moment suggestions, but you are deluding yourself if you think anyone is being fooled by your glibness.

Take advantage of such meetings by going to them well prepared. Most don't.

To go poorly prepared is to announce something about yourself, and to waste a unique opportunity. You are in the presence of your peers, perhaps your superiors. Conclusions will be made about your competence, dedication, creativity and aptitude for teamwork. If your associates see someone more interested in *bonhomie* than in making a contribution, you will have put a label of mediocrity on yourself that could limit your future progress.

Attend such meetings having given thought to the subject to be discussed and with carefully prepared suggestions to offer and you will have marked yourself as a person going somewhere.

That is the winning edge.

Enthusiasm—the energizer

People with the winning edge are people who love what they do.

If there is one dominant characteristic about leaders in any field, it is their enthusiasm. No dragging oneself out of bed and going to the office on leaden feet for them. Their eyes light up when they talk about their work. And their enthusiasm is infectious.

It is difficult, however, to be enthusiastic about your work if it doesn't challenge and excite you. So if your job is a drag, a burdensome responsibility dutifully assumed, think long and hard about staying with it. Ask yourself whether your job is worth your time. Give some thought to where success may take you. Look closely at the men and women who have reached the top in your field, the people who hold the positions, have the power and make the money you would like to make down the road. Will those achievements satisfy you when you reach that age? Would you like your life to be like theirs?

As the years go by, you and your responsibilities are going to grow. And as you grow you will be adjusting your sights. What satisfies you today may not in the tomorrows, and without an ever-expanding challenge, work that fulfilled you in the early years can become onerous and boring. Money is one thing; satisfaction is more important. Don't settle for some easily achieved goal; aspire.

Ask yourself: Is my job something I can do with enthusiasm? If you believe in what you are doing, if you are excited about it, and see it not as a job but as an opportunity—even as an adventure—you will almost certainly be successful. If you are bored with your work, or indifferent to it, you will almost certainly come short of your goals.

Give some thought to where success may take you.

Look closely at the men and women who have reached the top in your field, the people who hold the positions, have the power and make the money, you would like to make down the road. Will those achievements satisfy you when you reach that age? Would you like your life to be like theirs?

Be as sure as you can be that your job has enough potential to fulfill you. Don't settle for some easily achieved goal; aspire.

Remember: it may be unwise to set your sights too high; it is disastrous to peg them too low.

Expertise—the rare commodity

To achieve success in any field—whether it be managing a department, selling a product, teaching fitness, designing a space-station or breeding guppies—you need to know your subject.

The people who move ahead in the world of business, who have an edge over their fellows, are experts in their field. They know what the realities are, what the potential is and where the problems lie.

Determine to learn everything you can about the business you are in. Seek out the men and women who are leaders in your occupation. Read anything you can find that pertains to the subject. Look in the public library. Browse through the business section of a good bookstore. Ask a clerk to let you look at their copy of *Books in Print.*

Become an expert in your field. Aim at becoming *the* expert in your field.

The world is full of self-proclaimed experts, people who don't know what they are talking about but who fill the air with opinions. The way to rise above them is to know your stuff.

As a sometime television interviewer who has talked to hundreds of spokesmen and purported authorities on various subjects ranging from nuclear physics to gambling odds, I can tell you that it is as refreshing as a spring rain to meet a genuine specialist, a man or woman who is familiar with every aspect of his or her vocation and who can respond with quiet authority to the questions asked.

Knowledge is power. And knowledge derives from persistent thought, from reading, observing, questioning, studying, consulting and dreaming. And, of course, from experience.

Become an authority on what you do. Heads of companies everywhere are looking for and are prepared to reward men and women who know their stuff.

Taking time to think

To put it bluntly, the men and women with the winning edge in business use their brains.

Few of us take time to develop the mind. We set aside time for physical conditioning or for spiritual cultivation but we don't withdraw from our normal activities simply to think.

Do we think about our job? Of course we do. We resolve problems, make decisions and consult others. When we face a problem of consequence, we may cut off the telephone for a few minutes or close the door of the office to organize our thoughts. We may bone up on statistical data when we write a report or prepare for a staff meeting. At night we may even lie abed for a few minutes before sleep, reviewing the day and planning for the morrow.

But we don't set aside specific times in which to think, periods during which we examine, not just our immediate or pressing problems but our long-term objectives, our opportunities for personal and business growth, our future .

If I were asked to list the most valuable techniques for the achievement of success, high on the list would be the setting-aside of specific times to think. I know of no practice comparable in its benefits.

But thinking is hard work and there are many who take great pains to avoid it. We fail to realize that the human brain is an astounding instrument. Unlike most things, it doesn't wear out. Indeed, it improves with use. So put your brain to work; it will thrive on it. Treat it as you might your body when you begin a regimen of exercise. Ask it to do things it hasn't been doing. Discipline it.

And feed it, of course.

You will soon discover a new clarity of thought, a heightened imagination, fresh insights, better comprehension, expanding horizons and an exhilarating new zest for life. Your curiosity will be stimulated. New opportunities will become apparent at work, and you will have an enhanced ability to take advantage of them.

If your brain is lethargic, woolly, and imprecise, and if you are frequently bored, you are only half alive.

Get in shape intellectually; it will enlarge your life and give you that winning edge.

How? Read on.

The Think Tank

A friend of mine in Chicago, a prominent businessman known for his innovative approach to problems, has set up what he calls his "Think Tank." It is designed to help him deal with problems. It is a small, windowless, soundproofed, air-conditioned cubicle adjoining his office, a spartan place with only two items of furniture: a comfortable leather couch and a small table. On the table are a lamp and a dictating machine.

When he has a problem my friend withdraws to his Think Tank and lies down on the couch. His secretary guards against any intrusion. In total darkness and absolute silence he is free to concentrate on the question before him. As thoughts occur to him, he speaks into the dictating machine, his words to be transcribed later.

He withdraws for a few minutes each day to do one thing: to think about personnel problems, his product line, financial matters—anything and everything that particularly needs his attention. He attributes much of his success to the conclusions reached in his Think Tank.

My friend's technique may not appeal to you. But the practice of withdrawing to think is an important one, and its rewards are considerable.

Find a room where you can close the door and make clear that you are not to be interrupted—no easy achievement with small children who want to see Daddy.

Sit or stand or pace as it pleases you. Try lying down, although not, of course, if you are one of those who fall asleep the moment you are recumbent. The position will relax you, and the increased flow of blood to the brain contributes to clear thinking.

I have followed the practice for years. If, in working on a novel, for instance, I encounter plot problems or any of the numerous blocks that afflict writers, I stretch out on the carpet of my office for ten to fifteen minutes to ponder the dilemma. Do the problems get solved? Not automatically, of course. Sometimes not at all. But if I have wrestled with them and strained to resolve them and poured mental energy into them, "going to the mat" is oftentimes the catalyst.

Solving problems

How should you use your Think Tank to solve problems?

RULE ONE: It is a waste of time to wait, unfocused, hoping vaguely for some appropriate thought to happen by. This is the path to daydreams.

RULE TWO: Pose a specific problem to your imagination.

It is not enough to think in a general fashion; you must focus, as a jeweler does examining a diamond, looking at your problem from every angle. Investigate every facet of the problem: its nature, its various complexities, possible solutions. Think about the people involved and the financial implications. If your mind wanders, haul it back as you might a puppy you are training to walk on a leash.

Don't expect results after a once-over-lightly examination of your dilemma. But after you have thought about it, get up and go about your business. Put the problem out of mind. You have assigned it to your subconscious, where it is being worked on twenty-four hours a day. An answer will come.

If you have no pressing problems, use these moments of daily withdrawal as a way of inserting a period at the end of your workday. Review the day just concluded and formulate plans for the morrow. (More on this in Chapter 7, "How to Become an Innovator.")

You may be reluctant to adopt the technique, dismissing it as a gimmick. But follow the practice for a month. You will be surprised at the improvement in your daily performance, in the clearer perception of your job, in the better organization of your work, in the better execution of your responsibilities.

You will have a sense of being on top of your work, instead of feeling that you are forever chasing it. Even more important: you will find that you are beginning to come up with new ideas, procedures and approaches to your daily tasks.

Learning on the job

Interviewers often ask me, "How did you, with no experience in the newspaper business, become executive managing editor of the *Toronto Star* in sixteen months?"

The circumstances were unusual. I was beginning life over again at the age of forty-three, having spent two decades in the ministry. The publisher hired me, having observed my work on television, to produce the daily op-ed page, known on the *Star* then as Page Seven.

It was unfamiliar territory and I was, quite simply, at a loss. I knew nothing of the operation of a newspaper, never having so much as written an article for one. I did not know how to handle copy, lay out a page or write a headline.

But I was broke, needed a job and was bursting with ambition.

Within a few weeks of joining the paper I realized an important fact: that most of the staff did their work competently and professionally, but put the job out of mind at quitting time. They went home to their families or crossed the street to the Press Club to have a few beers and sit around shooting the breeze. Who could criticize this? Newspaper work is tough and demanding and they had earned their leisure.

Nor was their behavior unusual. The majority of men and women put their work out of mind when they leave the office. They are settled in the job, they know their trade, their future is secure and they are content with that.

But I had never been in the workaday business world and saw their "out of sight, out of mind" attitude as an opportunity. I committed myself to working long hours: twelve hours on weekdays, with lunch at my desk; Saturdays, until 1.00; Sunday mornings planning for the week ahead working hard to acquire the technical knowledge I lacked.

I was playing catch-up.

I learned to handle copy by taking stories from the composing room after they had been set in type, and studying how they had been processed.

Each day I took home copies of a half-dozen newspapers, Canadian and American, and studied them.

I took that nonpareil of headline writers, Willis Entwistle, to lunch and picked his brain.

I talked to the men in the engraving department and discovered a way to hasten a late-breaking photograph into the paper, enabling us to beat the opposition.

I had discussions with the foreman of the composing room, working out systems by which the editorial department and the composing room could work together more effectively.

On weekends I planned features and series and made various page layouts.

At each day's planning meeting I presented a half-dozen or more story ideas.

There were certain advantages: not knowing the rules, I wasn't bound by them. I could take unorthodox approaches. Did I make mistakes? Some dandies! There was much bemused head-shaking. There were caustic asides. Considering my neophyte status, a considerable degree of charity was shown.

To me there was no option: I had been given an extraordinary opportunity and I was determined not to blow it. I knew that success could only be achieved by a total commitment to the job.

That realization and the willingness to make that commitment provided the winning edge.

Sixteen months into the job, the executive managing editor's job came open. I got it.

FOR REVIEW

(1) Life is not what you find, it is what you create. You are born with existence and opportunity, and these are the raw materials out of which you can make a successful life.

(2) You cannot succeed without effort. If you want success badly enough and are prepared to work hard for it, there is every reason to believe you can have it.

(3) In the world of business, the difference between winners and losers is very small, but that difference is the winning edge.

(4) Prepare yourself for success. Expertise is a rare commodity and is in great demand.

(5) Few techniques for the achievement of success are as valuable as setting aside time to think. Use the Think Tank as a means to solve complex problems.

2 | Believing in Yourself

"**D**AY BY DAY, in every way, I'm getting better and better."
The words of Emil Coué, a French psychotherapist. They were repeated like a mantra by tens of thousands of men and women in England and the United States in the 1920s.

"Day by day, in every way, I'm getting better and better."

It was a prescribed routine. Men and women repeated the words at specified times of the day and whenever the thought crossed their minds. They believed that in so doing they were improving themselves, energizing themselves, equipping themselves for success in business and in life.

It was an early version of today's Positive Thinking and it had a tremendous vogue.

Emil Coué was not the first of his breed. His predecessors were numerous and included a man with the oddly appropriate name of Samuel Smiles, whose book, *Self-Help, with Illustrations of Character and Conduct*, was a best seller in Great Britain after its publication in 1859.

In 1908, Arnold Bennett, an English novelist and dramatist, published his *How to Live Twenty-four hours a Day*. Dozens of others followed, their various regimens offering happiness and success through applied psychology. They climaxed in the teachings of that high priest of religion-based self-help books, Norman Vincent Peale.

Peale, minister emeritus of the Marble Collegiate church in New York City, popularized the concept with his book, *The Power of Positive Thinking*, in the 1940s, and his followers and imitators soon proliferated.

The reverend Doctor's panacea is an admixture of truncated Christianity and pop psychology, a mélange of Biblical catch-phrases and simplistic self-help. It is presented, however, as an infallible technique for achieving success; infallible not least because it carries God's guarantee. Devotees are urged to affirm ten times a day the statement by the apostle Paul, "I can do all things through Christ which strengtheneth me," and are told, "Follow God's laws for success and you cannot fail."

Living limited lives

Positive thinking can be a useful psychological tool. It can also be illusory if you think you can talk yourself into success.

Too many people view life negatively. They see the glass half-empty rather than half-full. Say to them, "Isn't it a glorious day?", and they will respond, "Yes, but it looks like rain." Compliment them on a job superbly done and they are liable to respond, "Well, it's okay, I guess."

Some people seem negative by nature. Put a challenge before them and they will see the problems rather than the possibilities. They can look at anything and see only the flaws. I stood with a group in St. Peter's in Rome viewing Michelangelo's Pietà and heard a woman say she didn't like the way it was lit. They are the nay-sayers, the self-appointed inspectors of warts and carbuncles, charter members of The Noble Order of Mote-Removers and Neighbor-Judgers.

Years ago I bought a lot on Georgian Bay in Ontario's magnificent cottage country, intending to build on it. One weekend in late spring I took a friend north to show him the site. He looked at it, frowning.

"It's terribly isolated," he said.

"That's what I like about it; I want to get away from the city."

"You'll have to clear away a lot of trees."

"We'll use them. I'm going to build a log cabin."

"It'll cost you a packet to cut them down."

"I can burn them for years as firewood."

"But look at all the boulders; they'll have to be moved."

"I've hired a mason to build a fireplace."

"What will you do for water?"

"Pump it straight from the bay."

"You'll be snowed-in in winter."

"I won't be here in the dead of winter."

"Somebody will break in and steal your things."

"It's a hideaway. There won't be much worth stealing."

Nay-sayers' vocabularies are studded with "down" words: they speak of problems, frustration, failure, complications, trouble, obstacles, doubt, roadblocks, difficulties. They seldom dwell on challenge, solutions, opportunity, success, optimism, achievement, overcoming, hope, dreams.

Achievers are men and women who echo the theme in the children's book, *The Little Engine That Could.* "I think I can, I think I can."

Too often people put boundaries around their lives. Or they live within limitations imposed on them; usually by family or friends, sometimes by themselves. Raised with siblings they may have been overshadowed by older brothers or sisters. Their clothes were hand-me-downs. Their parents may have been scolds. Or indifferent. Or too busy to give them the love, the attention and the encouragement every child needs. As a consequence, they lack a sense of self-worth and find it difficult to express themselves and demonstrate their abilities.

Too many of us impose limitations on ourselves. We accept without question that certain goals are beyond us, that we can't hope to rise higher in life than our parents did, that we are slow to learn, that we lack the drive and the energy others have.

No matter how long you may have believed that you are fated to be what you are and that you cannot rise above it, you are wrong. You can improve your life measurably by altering your attitudes and your habits. Most of us are capable of achieving far more than we do, and we miss much in life by settling for less than we are capable of.

But first you must realize this. And you must glimpse the possible you.

There is an oft-told tale of a beggar who sat daily in the street across from an artist's studio. From his window the artist painted a portrait of the beggar and then one day called him in to see it. At first the beggar didn't recognize himself. Then, as recognition began to dawn, he asked, half-doubting, "Is that *me?* Can it be me?"

"That's the man as I see him," the artist replied.

The beggar studied the picture for a full minute and then said, "If that's the man you see, that's the man I'll be."

It is not facile sloganeering to assert that we can all be better than we are. The evidence is conclusive. There are ten thousand stories of men and women living below their potential who, by an act of will, set their feet on a better path.

Barbra Streisand is an artist of soaring talent. As a young woman aspiring to success in the theater and in films she faced two handicaps: she had a coarse Brooklyn accent and was not what is commonly thought of as beautiful. She went from theatrical agent to theatrical agent trying to get someone to represent her. They each turned her down, saying in effect, "*You*, a star! With that accent! And that nose!" She would rage at them: "You'll be sorry. Believe me, you will!" And they were, of course, for she became one of the great performing artists of our time.

But only because she scorned her disadvantages.

Can you rise above yours?

Living below your potential

Every day I see people with great potential who can't see it in themselves. They are doing passably well, but they themselves know they are achieving less than they could.

From time to time they get fired up with enthusiasm and dream of breaking out of the rut they are in. But they are slow to take the first step, and soon the dream dies and the plans abort and they continue on their middling way, failing to achieve what is clearly within their potential.

They continually make resolutions: "One of these days I'm going to do thus and so . . ." But the day never comes.

The fundamental problem is that they don't believe in themselves.

"Well and good," you may respond, "but how do I come to believe in myself? How do I go about changing for the better?"

To begin with, forget about running the 3.50 mile or becoming the chief executive officer or cornering the wheat market. Meet the challenge at hand. Don't set your sights on the top job but on the next job. You begin the journey to a distant city with one step.

All great achievements have simple beginnings. You begin to fly by lying on your back studying the flight of gulls at Kitty Hawk. You begin to invent the mass-produced automobile by running a bicycle repair shop in Dearborn, Michigan. You begin to discover the theory of relativity by learning your multiplication tables. You begin to write *Hamlet* by learning to write. You begin to compose the Fifth Symphony by practicing your scales.

The point is, of course, that "wishes won't make it so." You must act. You must take that first step. You must sit down and have a talk with yourself.

"How much do I want to succeed?"

"Do I have the resolution to commit myself to whatever it takes?"

"Is it possible for *me?*"

A moment's thought will make it clear that there have been many times in your life when, without making a great to-do about it, you have made the decision to alter an attitude or a pattern of behavior and have done so. The world is filled with people who, troubled by aspects of their lives, took action to change them:

- Millions have undertaken a fitness regimen to improve their health and have stayed with it.
- Millions of men and women have quit smoking.

- Millions of others have cut back on high-cholesterol foods and have permanently reduced their weight.
- Others have stopped ordering that double-martini for lunch or taking home that case of beer every Friday night.
- Still others have vowed to be kinder to a spouse or more thoughtful to a family member, or to spend more time with the children—and have done so.

As a result their lives have improved.

Such resolves undertaken and accomplished demonstrate that the making of a decision to improve oneself is not unusual; nor is carrying it out. It doesn't matter that in the past we may have failed to keep some of our pledges, the point is that, having recognized that we should change some aspect of our life, we have taken steps to do so and have achieved our goal.

The story of Helen Keller demands retelling here. Blind and deaf and dumb from infancy, her only intimations of the dark and silent world around her were through touch and taste and smell. So profound were her limitations that, it seemed, nothing could be done for her. How can you instruct someone who can't hear you? How do you know what her needs are when she can't tell you? How does she so much as know you are there when she can't see or hear you?

Helen Keller's spirit rebelled against the deprivation. Unable even to complain about or curse her fate, she could express her frustration only through tantrums and acts of violence against her parents and those around her. It seemed she was doomed to a life of silent hopelessness in an impersonal institution.

Then a remarkable young woman entered her life. I count her among life's great heroines. Her name was Anne Sullivan.

Helen Keller's parents hired her to handle the child whose isolation and anger had left them frustrated and despairing. Anne Sullivan, fully aware of the difficulties and of the apparent hopelessness of her task, nonetheless made a resolve to reach the child and to help her communicate with the world beyond herself. It was a battle against apparently impossible odds but she persevered, persevered over months of setbacks and discouragements that would have daunted the most courageous.

She simply rejected failure.

Then one day, unexpectedly, when disappointment had piled upon discouragement and it seemed success would never come, Helen uttered a single sound of comprehension. And, having made that first response, opened like a flower.

Tapped by another's faith in her, Helen Keller's potential poured forth. Slowly, painfully, stalled without progress at times, she went on to be honored finally in every country of the world as an author, lecturer and prime example of persistent courage. She could easily have done as one of Job's comforters suggested to him, "Curse God and die," but she chose otherwise. She chose to triumph over her handicaps rather than submit.

And, facing our relatively trivial disadvantages, so may we all.

The possible you

How can you come to believe in yourself?

Begin by looking around you. Are the successful people you know all that different from you in their basic abilities? Or have they merely done more with what they have? There are extraordinary men and women in our world, some of them geniuses, but the great majority are people very much like you who have simply applied themselves with a little more determination or worked a little harder or given a little more thought to their responsibilities and challenges.

Don't write yourself off . . .

- Because you never got beyond high school. I could fill this book with the stories of eminently successful men and women who never had the opportunity to go to college.
- Because you had a chance to succeed and blew it. Many achievers have blessed the day they failed in their early efforts; the failure opened doors they would not otherwise have approached.
- Because you are not prepossessing. Is there a physically less impressive woman alive than Mother Theresa but anyone more revered?

It is no vain faith to believe in yourself and in your potential, to picture yourself running the company rather than working for it, surpassing your peers, going beyond your dreams.

But first you must be able to see yourself doing it. You must come to believe in the possible you.

Idly sketching one rainy Sunday afternoon when I was twelve, I made a drawing of Felix the Cat, a popular comic strip character, and took it to my father. It was a rash thing to do, for each Sunday afternoon he retreated to what our family called the parlor with a variety of reading materials and a package of figs, closing the door behind him. He did not like to be interrupted.

But this Sunday afternoon he put his newspaper aside and looked carefully at the drawing. "Very good, Chuck," he said. "Was it done freehand?"

"Yes."

He studied the drawing, nodding approval while I trembled with excitement. My father almost never said a word of praise and seldom encouraged us five children. He returned the sketch to me and went back to his newspaper. "You have a talent for drawing," he said. "Keep it up."

From that day, I drew anything and everything that caught my eye. I filled up exercise books at school, indifferent to what was being taught.

After Dad left home, leaving the family to shift for itself, I mailed off sketches I thought might impress him and watched the mails for a reply. He seldom wrote, but when he did, any injection of praise stimulated me for weeks.

During the depths of the Great Depression, with my father gone and no money coming in except the welfare check, I had to leave school at seventeen. Stimulated by my father's spare comments, I made three drawings, portraits of Joe Primeau, Harvey "Busher" Jackson and Chuck Conacher, the famed "Kid Line" of the Toronto Maple Leaf hockey team and, without an appointment, took them to Mike Rodden, the then sports editor of the Toronto *Globe and Mail*. He hired me the following day. For the next four years I did a daily drawing for the *Globe* sports pages. It was my first job.

Visualize yourself succeeding

It is a fundamental maxim that, before beginning a journey, you must know where you are. You may have a destination in mind and a map, but unless you know where you are on the map it is impossible to take the steps necessary to get to your destination.

So, before you set out to reach your goals, undertake a personal inventory. Establish what your situation is and where you want to go. Do an unflinching self-examination. What is it about your attitudes, your commitment, your appearance or your background that limits your achievement? What are your skills and abilities and how much do they need to be upgraded?

One of the most effective ways by which you can change your life is through the technique of visualization. (You will find specific suggestions on how to do this in the following chapter, "The Magic of Self-Appraisal.")

Visualization is that act of the imagination by which you form mental images. It is seeing something in the mind's eye. The first objective will be to see yourself—literally see yourself—as you now are.

Begin by trying to visualize yourself in various specific situations. Conjure up a mental picture of yourself

- Busy at your desk or place of work.
- Greeting someone in the office.
- In conversation with the boss or a co-worker.
- Participating in a sales meeting.
- At lunch, talking business with a client.

Try to recall with deliberate objectivity your actions and attitudes in a recent business situation. What do you see? Do you see someone poised and reasonably self-assured or someone ill at ease? Does that person give an impression of self-confidence or does he or she hint of tentativeness, anxiety and a lack of self-assurance?

Now, change the picture. Attempt to visualize yourself in similar situations *the way you would like to be*. Then, determine to be that person. You may be helped in doing this by examining the way athletes use visualization to improve their performances.

I watched with fascination one of the high-jumpers at the Olympic games in Seoul. He was preparing himself for a record jump. On the television close-up you could see his lips moving as he talked to himself, the hint of body-English as he visualized the run-up to the bar, the flexing of the legs and the twisting of the torso as he thought his way through each sequence of the actual jump. A nod of confirmation and he was ready.

The camera moved in. You saw the concentration in the jumper's face. The jaw set as he lit his mental fuse. Then the long, bounding first steps, the increasing momentum, the thrust of the leg, the arching of the body and the triumphant clearing of the bar.

What had happened? The jumper had just cleared the height *twice*—once in his imagination and a second time before the crowd. The reason the actual jump went so well was that he had visualized it before it happened. He knew what was going to happen because he had seen it happen, in his mind.

"What pressure!" you exclaim. "He has this one chance and he has to make it work." Wrong. He had first seen it accomplished in his imagination and that gave him the confidence he could do it in reality.

Practicing visualization

Practice visualization. It has two benefits: it enables you to prepare yourself for a given situation and it is, in effect, a rehearsal. No theater company would put on a performance without having rehearsed it. A rehearsal is the living of an experience in advance. We have a saying, "Practice makes perfect," because, almost invariably, you perform better each time you do something.

Am I suggesting that all one has to do to accomplish any goal is to visualize it first? Of course not. The visualization must be preceded by preparation. The jumper could visualize his achievement only because he had prepared himself for it.

"But," you may object, "isn't this talk about visualization so much gobbledygook? The jumper doesn't need to visualize his achievement; he has acquired the ability to accomplish his goal through months of hard work."

No. Despite the training, and for all his ingrained skill, he is fully aware that in a given situation he can miss, and he must rid himself of that distracting doubt. By visualizing himself clearing the bar he reinforces his confidence and thus his performance. He is saying to himself: "I am capable of doing it. I have done it before. I will do it again."

Visualizing is simply a means of summoning your concentration and focusing it, of reminding yourself of what is true, of reinforcing that knowlege and then acting on it.

Visualization as preparation

I have a friend who has developed a procedure he follows whenever he has an important appointment—for illustrative purposes here, a business luncheon.

First, he prepares himself. He does his homework.

Second, he arrives early at the place of meeting.

He knows, as we all do, that nothing debilitates one's self-confidence more than arriving late for an important appointment. Because you are late you are likely to be unnerved and perspiring. Rather than being focused on the meeting you will be distracted, worried about how to justify your tardiness.

Consequently, my friend makes it a inflexible practice to arrive at the place of meeting ten minutes early. Rather than go directly to his table, he repairs to the public washroom, uses the urinal, washes his hands and checks his appearance. This done, his mind is freed of peripheral concerns and he is ready to focus his thoughts on the luncheon and its purpose.

He reviews the first names of the people he is about to lunch with so that he may use them in his greeting, exhales fully, draws a deep breath, consciously relaxes and visualizes himself approaching the table, greeting his associates, ordering lunch and, after a certain amount of small talk, broaching the subject to be discussed.

It hardly needs to be mentioned that his preparatory technique will not be effective if he has not done his homework and given consideration to the various directions the conversation may take.

Using the technique

How can you use the technique? Realize first that visualization is useless unless it is based on hard work. If you have failed to do the requisite preparation you will find it impossible to envision yourself succeeding.

If you find yourself hampered by feelings of inadequacy and often feel ill at ease in business or social situations, it is probable that you have not done the preparatory work to validate self-confidence. Nothing gives more confidence than knowing your stuff. Equip yourself for success and you you will discover the self-confidence you lack.

If a Helen Keller, with her disadvantages, can turn herself from a child hardly alive into a glowing, inspiring personality, can you not improve yourself?

Will it happen overnight? Of course not.

Will it happen if you put your mind to it? Of course.

It is no vain faith to believe in yourself and in your potential, to envision yourself running the company rather than merely working for it, surpassing your peers, succeeding beyond even your wildest dreams.

But first you must be able to visualize yourself doing it.

Reaching for new horizons

At the age of fifty-five I had never written a novel, nor had I plans to do so. I was at the time one of a consortium who had made an application for a cable television network license. A telephone call came from a friend in government informing me that our application would be rejected, and I was suddenly faced with the question, "What will I do with my future?"

Reviewing some files, I chanced upon a memorandum to myself, a dozen or so scribbled sentences outlining the plot for a motion picture. I sat in the silence of my office for some time asking myself whether I should pursue it further, finally picking up the telephone and calling an old friend, the novelist Arthur Hailey.

"Arthur," I said, "I have what I think is an unusual idea for a motion picture. How do I go about getting it into the hands of an agent or a producer, someone who can bring it into being?"

"Charles," he said, "the chances of success down that road are virtually nil. Even if you did find someone to take the idea and carry it through, the remuneration for what I gather is merely an outline wouldn't be all that much. Are you convinced that it's a really unusual idea?"

"Yes," I said.

"Then if you are—and, mind you, be sure you are—bet a year of your life on it. Develop it into a novel. If you can do that success-fully, you will earn income from the novel, and if it is a success, you may then be able to sell it to a film producer for a great deal more than you would get for the outline."

I put down the telephone and went for a long walk. Did I have the talent and the persistence to write a novel? I had written some non-fiction, but never a novel. As I thought about it, the conviction that I could do it grew within me. I saw myself doing the research, structuring the plot, developing the characters, beginning to write, polishing the prose...

I would bet a year on it.

One year and three months later the novel was finished. It was published in Canada by McClelland and Stewart, in the United States by Simon and Schuster and Avon Pocketbooks and in Great Britain, Italy, Holland, Japan and Argentina. Subsequently it was made into a motion picture, *The Kidnapping of the President*, star-ring William Shatner, Hal Holbrook, Ava Gardner and Van Johnson. I have since written five novels.

Am I saying that anyone can achieve anything simply by high resolve, unremitting commitment and old-fashioned hard work? Of course not. But granted the desire, the dedication and the capacity to visualize yourself succeeding at what you have committed your-self to, you can achieve far more than you might dream possible.

FOR REVIEW

(1) Success cannot be achieved through psychological pep-talks and slogans; hard work and imagination are required.

(2) Ascertain your potential through a thoroughgoing self-appraisal. Avoid negative thinking and don't put limitations on your dreams.

(3) Try to glimpse the possible you. Are the successful people you know all that different from you in their basic abilities?

(4) Learn to use the technique of visualization. Observe how athletes use it. Visualization enables you to see yourself as you are, and as you can be.

(5) Stop putting limitations on yourself and begin to live up to your potential.

3 | The Magic of Self-Appraisal

YOU HAVE AN APPOINTMENT with the president of a corporation for which you would like to work. He leans across his desk and says, "If we were to employ you, what would you bring to us? And give me the bad with the good."

How would you respond? What qualifications *do* you bring to the marketplace?

Any organization that markets a product takes regular inventories. By taking stock, the company updates itself on what it has to sell, what is in short supply and whether some of its merchandise has become outmoded.

Individuals, too, need to take stock from time to time. Ask yourself: "What are my particular talents and skills? Am I equipped to compete with my peers? Am I prepared to spend the time and thought and energy it takes to succeed? Is it possible that some of what I know has become outmoded?"

"Know thyself," said the philosopher. The best way to do that is to stand apart from yourself, to evaluate yourself as a stranger might. Then, scrutinizing yourself as objectively as you can, to assess your abilities and recognize your shortcomings.

Someone may object, "But this is a pointless exercise. I already know myself. Doesn't everybody?"

The answer is, "No!" We are all given to some self-delusion; we are all disposed to rationalize our weaknesses and justify our failures.

Too many of us of us believe we are better than we are. We believe the principal reason we haven't done better in our career is that we haven't gotten the breaks. We stubbornly refuse to face unpalatable truths about ourselves: such things, perhaps, as our lack of commitment, our tendency to procrastinate, our short attention span, our shirking of onerous duties, other things.

Others of us, on the other hand, believe we are worse than we are. We lack self-confidence. We feel inadequate. We duck difficult challenges because we don't want to fail. As a consequence, we doom ourselves to mediocrity.

We are all too ready to settle for second-best.

Let's have done with such self-delusion. Pause now to take a hard look at yourself. What do you bring to the marketplace?

Realize before you begin, however, that anyone who can answer all of the following questions affirmatively would be a halo-encircled paragon. The point of the exercise is not to pass an examination but to do a stocktaking, to make an inventory of what you bring to the marketplace. And then, having isolated your strengths and weaknesses, to take whatever action may seem wise.

Deal with each question honestly, knowing that to delude yourself is to betray yourself.

Analyzing your abilities

Are you industrious?
Or are you given to laziness? Do you put the job out of mind when you leave the office? Do you seldom stay late or take work home or go to the office weekends when you have fallen behind? Do you take more coffee breaks than others, and do you waste time in idle chatter about extraneous matters? Do you sleep late weekends, excusing it by saying, "I need more sleep than others"? Would you

rather sit around and talk than read that book you know you should read? Do you waste most evenings in front of the television set? Do you resolve to keep yourself fit and then, when it becomes hard work, let things slide? If you had to describe yourself in either of two words would that word be industrious or lazy?

Are you ambitious?

Yes, of course, you want to get ahead, but do you really work at it? Are you taking specific steps to improve your abilities, to hone your skills, to better equip yourself? Have you established goals for yourself? Are you pursuing them in such a way as to meet your timetables? Have you set your sights on specific career accomplishments? Have you laid plans to achieve them? Are your aspirations as high as they should be? Are you aiming for a mere raise in pay or a minor promotion when you should be shooting for a senior management role, even a vice-presidency?

Are you disciplined?

Knowing what you have to do, do you do it? Or are you a procrastinator? If you have a responsibility to meet, something onerous and unrewarding, do you sigh but nonetheless get on with it and persevere until it is done? Or do you tend to postpone it and then do it in a final pell-mell rush?

Are you organized?

Is your work untidy to the point of shambles or do you "plan your work and work your plan"? Not having a secretary, do you maintain your own files and keep them up to date? Could you, if required to, lay your hands on any given document on a minute's notice? Do you have a corner at home where you keep an active file as an adjunct to the one at the office? Do you makes notes to yourself or do you usually trust your memory? Do you maintain a pocket calendar and a detailed one at work and consult them first thing each day? Do you, at the first opportunity, enter important dates and events in your calendar, or do you postpone doing so? Do you frequently forget appointments or deadlines and then panic trying to catch up? Do you find yourself playing catch-up frequently?

Are you creative?
Are you good at solving problems? Do you welcome them? If you are assigned a task, do you tend to follow standard procedures or do you look for better ways to accomplish it? Faced with a problem, do you get bogged down in analyzing it, or do you quickly move to assess it and start questing about for solutions? If a piece of equipment breaks down, what is your automatic reaction — to turn up the original invoice and reorder it, or to decide to find out what's new in the field that might do the job better? Are you exasperated when systems fail but nevertheless continue to work within them? Or do you set out to change them? Are you a contributor to the Suggestion Box or do you never give it a thought?

Are you focused?
Do you take pains to define your goals and then stay with them? Do you tend to think of a dozen things at once? Are you given to enthusiasms and then a cooling of interest? Is your mind on your job or do you do a lot of daydreaming? Do you lack drive? Are you stirred by vague ambitions but not quite sure how to get moving? If there is a task to be done, do you get right to it? Do you keep wondering if perhaps you should change jobs but never fully make up your mind either to stay or to go?

Are you honorable?
Do you usually tell the truth even when you know you can get away with warping the facts? Do you exaggerate your accomplishments and dismiss your failures? Do you put down others of whom you are jealous? Do you cut corners, bend the truth, slant your responses, take credit that isn't legitimately yours, mislead by silence, misrepresent what you know to be the facts? Do you cheat on your spouse? Do you rig your expense accounts or your income tax returns?

Are you a realist?
Do you believe that one of these days you are going to get that big break even though you know you don't really rate it? Do you have enough hard sense realistically to evaluate your skills and your

potential? Are you open-eyed enough to know that there are certain aspirations you cannot hold without inevitably falling short, while at the same time recognizing that what you lack in certain areas you more than make up for in others? Are you well aware of your limitations and your strengths? Have you been answering the questions in this questionnaire with candor or have you been glossing over the difficult ones?

Ask yourself the fundamental question: Why do I want to succeed? — rearranging the order of the following statements to reflect your priorities.

- I want to succeed because, in business, success is the name of the game.
- Succeeding is a matter of personal pride.
- I want to succeed for the sake of my family.
- I want the approval of my peers.
- I want the rewards: money, power and authority.

Taking a closer look

In doing your self-analysis, try the approach of a religious on a retreat.

Find a solitary place. Get away from telephones and family and possible interruptions. Find refuge, if need be, in the attic or the basement or the garage or wherever. Drive your car to a quiet place or to a lonely side road. If in a city, park in the lee of a factory that is quiet on a weekend. It doesn't matter where, as long as you are able to concentrate.

As you begin, have a Dutch-uncle talk with yourself. This moment could be a watershed in your life.

Begin by reviewing the questions listed at the beginning of this section: Are you industrious? Are you ambitious? Are you disciplined? Are you organized? Are you creative? Are you focused? Are you a realist? Are you honorable?

Don't merely reread the questions; deal with them one by one. Make notes of your responses to each question.

For example, under the category, "Am I industrious?", you may write something like: *"Not nearly industrious enough. Stop sleep-*

ing late on weekends. Cut back on television—one hour max. Plan each week's work agenda early Sunday mornings. Discipline! Discipline! Discipline!"

You get the idea.

When you have finished, reduce your notes to a single page and post it where it can serve to jog your memory. (The inner surface of a clothes-closet door is a good place; you'll see it each morning.)

Tell your spouse about your resolve. It will help to deepen your determination; you won't want to fail in front of your partner.

As you begin the new regimen, there is a fundamental question you must ask yourself: "Am I prepared to work as hard as will be needed to achieve my goals?

Let this be stated unequivocally as the fundamental fact about success: *Apart from extraordinary talent, nine times out of ten, success is directly attributable to one thing: hard work.*

It is not all that difficult for ambitious people to succeed in business, because most of the people in any organization give less than their best to the job.

Most of them much less!

If you are prepared to "go the second mile," you are almost certain to move up the ladder.

Merely putting in extra hours will not suffice. It is not enough to take home work that did not get finished during business hours. The time we are discussing is time beyond the requirements of duty, creative time.

Appraising yourself

Let us continue our quest to improve ourselves by doing an unflinching appraisal of our personality traits.

It is not an easy thing to do. Robert Burns wrote:

Oh wad some power the giftie gie us,
To see oursels as others see us.

Unfortunately, in looking at ourselves, most of us tend to see "through a glass darkly." Looking at others' faults we peer through the magnifying lenses of the binoculars; looking at our own we do the reverse.

But what we will try to do here is to look candidly at our pluses and our minuses, the good and the bad.

Here is a test by which you may conveniently examine yourself. Begin by getting a number of sheets of paper and copying the following checklist, leaving space beneath each category for your comments:

Appearance
Face? Body? Hair? Posture? Mannerisms? Clothes? Sense of Style?
Hypothetically, your response here might read like this:

Face? Passable. No film star but then I still get some looks.

Body? In good shape, but then I work out every morning.

Hair? Beginning to thin but there's nothing I can do about that; my old man is bald. Needs shampooing more often, though.

Posture? I tend to slump, standing up and sitting down. Makes me look like a slob. Must stop it.

Mannerisms? Nothing too objectionable, although I've been told I talk with my hands too much.

Clothes? Definitely needs to be worked on. Yes, I'm careless sometimes, but laundry and dry-cleaning costs a bundle these days!

Sense of style? Okay, maybe I do carry "casual" too far. There have been a couple of smart-ass comments about it lately, but if I do my work what difference does it make? The roof would fall in if I arrived at the office wearing a tie and jacket . . .

The first category responded to, move on to the others. Don't just give the exercise a casual scrutiny, work at it. Try to see yourself as others see you. Look for aspects of your personality, your manner and your attire that need improvement. Concentrate, and don't delude yourself.

Ambition
Doer? Dreamer? Planner? Go-getter? Procrastinator? Driven? Goal-setter? Vacillator?

Education
Formal? Informal? Adequate? Lacking? Find study difficult?
Anxious to learn? Reading habits? Do I strive to learn?

Personality
Pleasing? Forbidding? Open? Shy? Energetic? Restrained?
Easygoing? Negative? Retiring?

Energy
Abundant? Lacking? Widely fluctuating? Tire easily? Sleeping
habits good? Daily diet balanced?

Leadership ability
Confident? Timid? Able to inspire? Good judge of character? Too
assertive? Tactful? Quick study? Ready to share credit?

Ability to communicate through speech
Excellent? Average? Inadequate? Vocabulary limited? Articulation
sloppy? Slow thought processes?

Ability to communicate through writing
Vocabulary lacking? Spelling weak? Grammar deficient? Trouble
organizing thoughts? Handwriting poor? Able to type? Able to use
wordprocesser?

Creative skills
Original thinker? Good imagination? Enjoy solving problems?
Don't know how to start? Give up easily? Thoughts disorganized?

Ability to work with others
Cooperative? Good organizer? Resent superiors? Like people?
Need to lead? Quarrelsome? Peacemaker? Stubborn? Dominant?
Demand appreciation?

Cooperativeness
Contentious? Equable? Self-assertive? Accommodating?
Dominant? Obstinate? Arbitrary? Friendly? Easily hurt?

Conciliatory? Enjoy others' triumphs?

Using the checklists

It will do no good merely to scan the two self-analysis checklists and then pass on. Concentrate through one entire day on each of the categories.

I am not proposing that you set aside an entire day to think about each one—you have other obligations. Simply do this: Decide that all day Monday, say, you are going to maintain, just below the surface of your mind, the questions asked under the category: *Ability to communicate through speech*. Now, observe yourself as you move through the day. Focus on your ability, or inability, to communicate well. You will be astonished at how revelatory it will be. Through the activities of the day you will frequently find yourself evaluating your skills or lack of them. The analysis may even intrude when you are concentrating on other things: when you are talking on the telephone, involved in a staff meeting, having lunch with associates or watching television in the evening.

Follow the same pattern on Day Two, focusing on another category, and on each succeeding day. Let the part of your personality you are analyzing overarch your day. Do the same on the remaining days. At the end of the time you will know more about yourself than you ever have.

You might ask your spouse, a family member or a friend how they would rate you in certain areas. Ask for candor. Discount obvious flattery but don't bristle if you get answers that don't please you.

It could be a disheartening experience, and discouraging. But don't let that deter you. Remind yourself that the point of the exercise is to do a thoroughgoing personal inventory. With the knowledge you gain you will move forward.

Think of the your self-appraisal as moving day.

When you are preparing to move from one house to another, you evaluate everything you possess. You decide what needs to be discarded and what you will keep.

On moving day you realize how much useless junk you have accumulated. You linger over memories and make reluctant judgments. Finally, you discard much of your past and go off to the new environment, exhausted by the experience but filled with hope and expectation.

So it is with your self-appraisal. Before moving on to better things, undertake a critical examination of the baggage you carry with you. Take a long, hard look at yourself. See yourself as you are and as others may see you. Then begin to make changes.

You may find that you have listed more negatives than positives. But you will also know who you are and where you are in life. You will be able to see the path you must take to achieve your goals.

One guarantee: You will find the exercise both intimidating and exhilarating.

Making changes

When the appraisal is done, go to work on yourself.

Don't try to correct everything at once; you'll be overwhelmed, grow discouraged and quit. Use a laser, not a shotgun. Tackle a relatively easy problem first. You'll achieve it and draw encouragement from the experience for the next step. With a victory under your belt, go on to a more difficult problem.

A word of common sense: If you believe that a week Friday you'll have it made, forget it. You have built your bad habits and ingrained your weaknesses over a lifetime. They won't yield in a day.

If you are determined to succeed in business, there is a further price to be paid: a cutting-back on your social life.

Man has been defined as a social animal. We need friends. Friends make life more interesting, more rewarding.The deepest attachments of life are with members of the opposite sex and with our children, but we need associations beyond our immediate family. There is a camaraderie among men of kindred spirit, an openhearted sharing among women that is unique. And essential.

But one of the great threats to achievement is to have too many friends, to be too social. Friendships are important but they can co-opt time that should be dedicated to your work.

Pleasurable as it may be, an overly active social life can militate against your success. It can eat into your weekends—times when you need to study or do some planning or work at various projects.

Partying weeknights—unless you are disciplined about saying no to that second or third drink and about heading home at a reasonable hour—will diminish your mental acuity and sap your creativity the following day.

We are all familiar with the phrase, "the morning after."

Examining your appearance

Let me introduce you to four people. Take note of your initial reaction to them.

The first is a man dressed in a black pin-striped three-piece suit. He is wearing a white-on-white shirt and a conservative silk tie. He has three rings on his fingers and is paunchy.

The second is a woman in a skintight split skirt and a low-necked blouse. Her hair is blond and bouffant and her jewelry is flashy. She tends to look at you from the corners of her eyes.

The third is a man who, at the earliest opportunity, shucks off his jacket to reveal, beneath a tight, short-sleeved shirt, the sloped shoulders and knotted muscles of a bodybuilder. At the first opportunity he injects into the conversation the fact that he has just finished his daily workout at his health club.

The last is a middle-aged woman in a tweed suit and sensible shoes. Her graying hair is gathered back in a loose chignon. Her wristwatch has a cloth band and her horn-rimmed glasses are attached to a black ribbon.

On the ground of my brief descriptions have you not already come to some conclusions about these people?

We may say that we take people as they come but isn't it a fact that we are influenced by our first impressions?

How many times have you heard it said, "You know, she's really a wonderful person when you get to know her"?

It may take weeks before that initial conclusion is revised; in the meantime, that person must overcome the negative impression she has already made.

Making a first impression

Are first impressions important?

- Ask the theatrical producer as he plots the action and the lighting for when the curtain goes up on Act One.
- Ask the architect who is making the drawings for the foyer of a new $100-million building.
- Ask anybody who ever went out on a blind date.

Do first impressions matter? Whether we like it or not, the answer must be an unequivocal yes.

Snap judgments about people are often unfair. Bad taste sometimes camouflages good character. But would we want a world in which everyone dressed and behaved like everyone else? It may be useful in the armed forces but not in daily life. Uniformity is depressing. It smacks of regimentation.

It is nevertheless important to realize that your clothes and your manner do communicate something to others, and that what they conclude about you may work to your advantage or disadvantage.

It is not unreasonable in a customer-oriented business for the boss to insist on a certain standard of attire. If the business is banking, say, and the teller sports a three-day growth of beard and unkempt hair, and wears a peak cap at work, who could blame a maiden aunt for having second thoughts about trusting him with her money?

You may deliberately choose to flout the code. Some will commend your independence of spirit, others will wonder at your judgment. I am advocating neither course; I am simply speaking to the realities of business life in most companies.

There are eminently successful men who come to work in jeans, a T-shirt and sandals. Others consider a white shirt, a tie and a vest *de rigeur*. Wear what you will, but be aware that the visual impression you present will often work to your advantage or disadvantage.

When I lived in Princeton, New Jersey, I was on my way from the campus to town one day, when I saw what I took to be an old bag-lady shuffling along the sidewalk in front of me. She was wearing a shapeless gray overcoat. Her trousers sagged over scruffy boots. A woolen toque was pulled low over her head, and from beneath it, rusty, platinum hair pushed out untidily. As I overtook her, she stopped, stepped off the wide sidewalk, pulled off the toque and bowed in a courtly, old-world manner.

Albert Einstein!

I was so taken aback at recognizing the great nuclear scientist that I hardly returned his *Guten morgen*.

We often passed in the street in the three years I lived there. He was teaching at the Institute for Advanced Study and lived in a house nearby. Einstein was a sartorial spectacle. His unlaced shoes flapped as he walked. He wore no socks. His baggy trousers were secured with a knotted rope. He habitually wore a gray crewneck sweater over a flannel shirt, and in cooler weather, a woolen toque. When a journalist asked him why he wore no socks he replied that socks got holes in them. When asked why he removed his hat when it rained, he said it was easier to dry his hair than his hat.

An Einstein can be indifferent to clothing; most others can't.

Your body language

In appraising yourself, remember that we communicate, not only through our attire, but through what is sometimes called "body language."

Notice how often people seek to say something by their manner.

Some men feign an overpowering vigor. The voice is loud and assertive. Your hand is seized in a macho grip and pumped. The smile is turned on and, just as swiftly, off. Other men are diffident to the point of unfriendliness. Some men carefully repeat your name and the off-focus of their eyes tells you that they are entering it in a card-file. Some look down at you in cool appraisal, as a horse-trader might look at a yearling. There are men who don't trouble to rise from their chairs to say "Hello," but give you an indifferent wave; others are so obsequious they remind you of Uriah Heep.

There are women who strive to appear businesslike and efficient by adopting an officious manner. Still others affect mannish attire, even lowering their voices.

The point is this: by his or her demeanor, each person is seeking to transmit information about himself or herself.

What signals do *you* send?

It is important to know. You ought not to tailor your personality to the expectations of others, but you should be aware of what is being perceived by the person you are meeting for the first time; indeed, by those who know you well and work with you daily. And because there is no point in handicapping yourself by creating bad impressions, impressions that may take weeks or months to undo, take a look at yourself.

Is your dress eccentric? Do you simulate an interest in others that you don't feel? Do you have a tendency to smile ingratiatingly? Have you perfected little mannerisms designed to draw attention to yourself? Do you convey that you have more to teach than to learn? Do you move toward other people or do you wait for them to come to you? Are you overbearing? Do you interrupt others, feeling that what you have to say is more important?

If you employ any of these or other stratagems, you are probably not getting away with them. Because most of us are not trained actors, our tactics will be obvious. You might be surprised at how transparent your power-moves are and how many of your associates trade winks when they see you turning them on.

Such maneuvers may occasionally accomplish what they are intended to; more often than not, they will alienate.

You are a worthwhile person, are you not? Then why not be yourself? Most people are impressed by naturalness and genuineness; there is no need to try to slip up on their blind side.

FOR REVIEW

(1) "Know thyself." It is perhaps the best counsel to be given to anyone who aspires to move upward in the marketplace. Take the time to take stock.

(2) Be specific in your self-analysis: Are you industrious? Are you ambitious? Are you disciplined? Are you orga-

nized? Are you creative? Are you focused? Are you honorable? Are you a realist?

(3) Ask yourself the basic question: Are you prepared to work as hard as will be necessary to achieve your goals? Nine times out of ten, success is directly attributable to one thing: hard work.

(4) We make preliminary judgments about others based on first impressions. Others make similar judgments about us. It may be some time before that initial impression is revised.

(5) We communicate without words; not only through our attire but through body language. What signals do you send?

(6) Most people are impressed by naturalness and genuineness, so be yourself.

4 | Don't Like Your Job? Change It

I‌T HAS BEEN MY OBSERVATION that a great many men and women — probably a majority — dislike their work.

Each day they keep an eye on the clock until quitting time. Each week they mutter, "Thank God it's Friday!"

They dislike their working conditions. They hate the hours. They gripe about the management. They're not satisfied with the money. They worry about their future.

They would, they say, give anything to change jobs.

Why do so many people work at jobs they are bored with or dislike?

There are many reasons, of course, but usually it's because their vocations were determined years earlier by parents or guidance counselors or chance. They're in the business they're in because it's the business they began in. The present job is the extension of the first job, and with the passage of the years they have gotten into a rut.

A friend of mine, a married man in his late thirties who has been in the work force for fourteen years, confided that he disliked his job and would give anything to change it, but he feared that it was now too late.

I pointed out to him that, with male life expectancy now in the mid-70s, he could reasonably expect to live another forty years and work for another thirty. His life was not half over; he had two-thirds of his working years ahead of him. Yet he was ready to accept an extended serfdom because it was, he said, "too late to change."

Madness.

As was pointed out in the Introduction, our days break roughly into three periods: we spend eight hours at work, we sleep for eight hours and we have eight hours in which to do as we please. Half our waking hours are spent at work.

To permit half of your conscious life to be wasted in some soul-destroying drudgery is to act the fool.

Worse, disliking your job almost guarantees that you will do it poorly. You won't give it the time and concentration it needs. Your resentments will diminish your drive, sap your energy and dry up your creative juices. There are tens of thousands of men and women in the business world whose potential is not and will not be realized simply because they dislike their work and therefore lack incentive.

Robert Frost wrote:

My object in living is to unite
My avocation and my vocation
As my two eyes make one in sight.
Only where love and need are one
And the work is play . . .
Is the deed ever really done

. . .

Fear in the face of change

Why do most of those who would like to change their job fail to do so? The answer is usually fear or inertia.

They are afraid to release the bird in the hand for fear there won't be another one — never mind two — in the bush. They are intimidated, as everyone is in some measure, by fear of the unknown. It is my view that most such fears about changing one's job are groundless. Moreover, if you have decided to play it safe you have made a fundamental decision: you have decided to stop growing.

Fear is not reprehensible. It is a valid emotion. It is nature's way of preserving us from a perceived danger.

In nature, there are three reactions to fear: flee, freeze and fight.

In the presence of danger, some creatures *flee*.

The bird takes wing, the impala bounds away, the fingerling darts from the jaws of the bass. Flight enables them to preserve their lives, but it means a life controlled by others, a life of reaction rather than action.

In the presence of danger, some creatures *freeze*.

They seek to make themselves invisible in the hope that the threat will go away. They, in effect, cross their fingers, hold their breath and hope for the best.

In the presence of danger, some creatures *fight*.

They will not permit the enemy to determine their fate. They will resist to the best of their abilities.

Humans react in the same ways. Faced with the uncertainties implicit in changing jobs, we experience fear. This is a normal reaction; we are all afraid of the unknown. In the face of our fears we have three options. We can run away, we can ignore the problem and freeze, or we can gather our courage and fight.

But surely the fear of an unknown tomorrow must be measured against a more legitimate fear — the fear of spending the remainder of your life at some unrewarding or demeaning or debilitating task. Added to which there is the very real possibility that, if you fail to take action, your subsequent resentment of your lot in life may adversely affect your disposition and your health.

Some people are deterred from taking action to change their job by the fear of making a major mistake. The job they now have may not be everything they might like it to be, but things could be worse. If they do gather their courage and make a jump, can they be sure that the parachute will work?

It's a matter of the devil they know and the devil they don't know.

Fear of the unknown

Be reassured by the fact that it is normal to suffer trepidation in the face of change. John Milton said, "Fear of change perplexes monarchs." Life is more comfortable when it is predictable. There is a sense of security in the familiar.

A radical change in the direction of your life is no trivial thing. It creates uncertainty. It involves risk. But, if you decide, after sober thought, that you should make a change, delay only compounds your problem. Might the change be a mistake? Of course it might — life offers few certainties. The only people who don't make mistakes are in the cemetery.

In addition to the problem of fear, there is the problem of inertia. In physics, inertia is the tendency of an object to remain in the condition it is in. If it is motionless it resists moving. If it is in motion it resists a change in direction or velocity. Inertia can be altered only by a force greater than the tendency to remain as is.

The law of inertia applies also to the mind.

To change the pattern of life takes an act of will. It requires a wrench and a jerk. It is not enough to think wistfully about the need to change your job; you will remain as you are unless you summon your resolve, persevere in your determination and then act.

That initial action is exceedingly difficult to take. Carl Lewis, the American sprinter who won four gold medals at the 1984 Olympics, said of the hundred-meter dash, "The effort needed to reach full speed is greater than that needed to maintain that speed."

I have a friend, a talented and capable man. He has a good, well-paying job, but he scorns the work he does as trivial (it is) and is constantly talking about moving to another job. He is successful at what he does, so he has opportunities to change jobs, but the other jobs are similar to the one he has, and if he makes a change he will soon find himself in the same situation he is now in. Despite this, when other promising options are pointed out to him, he becomes evasive and changes the subject.

What he does is working for him: it pays well, he can do it easily and his future is reasonably secure. Nevertheless, he feels demeaned by his job, and for all his financial success he is an unhappy man. It isn't so much that he chooses to stay with what he is doing as it is that he avoids choosing to do something else.

His name is legion.

Another friend has a good position in a business that has no future. In some jobs, there is nowhere to go but up. In others there *is* no up. If your company manufactures buggy whips or coal furnaces or iceboxes, you would be well advised to study the help-wanted ads.

If the business isn't going anywhere, neither are you.

Is your restiveness real?

So you are prepared to change jobs and ready to make a choice. Fine. Before you do so, however, a word of caution.

Be dead certain that you should. Make sure you are fundamentally unhappy or unfulfilled in your work and not merely restive.

Make certain that your discontent does not stem from the fact that you are passing through a period of general dissatisfaction with the way your life is moving.

It may be that your disquietude arises from some personal problem: you have, perhaps, gotten in over your head financially, or your marriage is in trouble, or something else is eating at you.

It may be that something has happened to make you aware of your limitations. Perhaps you have concluded that you aren't, as you once fondly believed, a world-beater, and this realization has shaken you.

It could be that friends and former classmates are making more progress in their careers than you are, and this has induced resentment and a formless, brooding anger.

It is possible that you haven't been giving your best to the job and that your restlessness is an outgrowth of a dissatisfaction with yourself.

It may be that there is a personality clash between you and a superior, and that you know, in moments of candor, the fault is as much yours as his.

It could be that, as William Shakespeare has Cassius say in *Julius Caesar*: "The fault, dear Brutus, is not in our stars,/ But in ourselves." Or as an anonymous Quaker said to his wife:

Everyone is wicked save thee and me.
And sometimes I wonder about thee.

If the problem is you rather than the job, go slowly before you make a move. We carry our baggage with us.

Going into business for yourself

Is it possible that your restiveness at work arises from the fact that you are not well suited temperamentally to working for others?

You don't fit into routines. You react adversely to being told what to do. You like to work at your own pace, and the very nine-to-fiveness of most jobs irritates you.

You would like to be on your own.

Perhaps, then, you should consider starting your own business. If your goals are wealth and independence, owning your own business may be the best route to them. Look around you. The financially independent are mostly men and women who sell a product or a service. They don't work for others, they work for themselves. They are the employers rather than the employees.

And they are not necessarily the ablest people in the society. Your observation will have told you that.

They have discovered that they can make available something other people want. They have done the hard, slogging work required to start and establish a new business.

But before you begin to investigate the possibility of becoming an entrepreneur, give thought to the rules that are fundamental to creating a new business enterprise.

- You must have something to sell or must provide some service that people will pay money to receive.
- You must be prepared to work twelve- to sixteen-hour days and at least six days a week until you are established.
- You must have in hand enough capital or enough assured credit to get you through the first year and set you on the threshold of the next.
- You must guard against the temptation to expand too quickly,

but have enough guts to take a giant step if the opportunity comes.

If you are prepared to accept these conditions and have access to sufficient capital, investigate the possibilities. You might wish to consider the purchase of a franchise. (But remember: the franchise world is full of smooth-talking flimflam men.)

Keep your critical faculties sharp.

Before you decide to start your own business, ask yourself a further question: Am I sufficiently self-disciplined and self-reliant to step out on my own?

Your response may be: "I have it in me to be disciplined. The reason I am sometimes indifferently so and occasionally lazy is that I haven't had a proper incentive." That may well be, but before you take the plunge, satisfy yourself that you are temperamentally suited to independence.

People who want to work for themselves must realize that they must take full responsibility for:

• The financing and management of the venture
• The production of the product or service being offered
• The merchandising of the product or service.

You will have no one but yourself to supervise your activities, to correct your mistakes or to inspire or goad you.

There will be no one but you to blame if things go wrong.

The entrepreneurial role is a tough one, but it can be rewarding. If you are an individualist who doesn't work well in harness, and if you have the self-discipline required to accomplish your goals, then plan carefully and have a go.

The prerequisites are imagination, a belief in yourself and lots of self-discipline. Can you dream dreams and then bring them down to earth? Can you, when there is no one to require you to, haul yourself out of bed on a bad morning to go to your office or shop and, even when you don't feel like it, put your head down and do your job?

If you can, you are over the big hurdle. If you can't, forget it.

Before you commit yourself to a new career, whether it be your own business or simply a change of job, assure yourself that it has the potential to challenge and reward you through a lifetime. The job may not endure that long, for these are times of accelerating change, but it may. Remember the old French proverb: "Be careful what you set your heart on, for you will surely get it."

Perhaps you aren't as unhappy in your work as you think at the moment. The story is told of Colette, the famed French novelist and performer, that she once watched her life story as it was portrayed on the screen.

A friend said, "It looks as though you had a happy childhood."

"Yes," Colette replied, "It's too bad I didn't realize it at the time."

Preparing the mind

There is one further question: Are you intellectually prepared to move into a better situation? Or do you need to take some time off to prepare yourself for the future? Are there, for instance, deficiencies in your education? Have your basic skills become outdated? Should you take a special course in some branch of the computer sciences? Even go back to school?

"Back to school!" you say. "Good god, man. I graduated ten years ago!"

A lot has happened in the business world since most business executives were in school. The song says, "The world she is a-changin' " — yes, and at supersonic speeds. It has been estimated that knowledge now doubles every ten years. If you want to change jobs, maybe you need to learn a new skill.

I am not suggesting that everyone return to full-time study; there are extension courses available in every city of any size. There is night school. There are correspondence courses. Check with the education department or the appropriate government office in your city. There is more help available than you might imagine.

I have pointed out some pitfalls — erring perhaps on the side of too many cautions — but don't let that lead you too easily to surrender your dream of changing jobs.

As I write I am thinking of an acquaintance, a man in his mid-thirties. He was a star athlete in college and an A student. He had his mind set on a medical degree, and if ever there was a man born to practice medicine it was he. He devoured medical journals, sub-scribed to various professional publications and was a walking pharmacopoeia. To mention that you were not feeling well was to be the subject of an on-the-spot diagnosis.

Unfortunately, he had to break off his pre-med studies for lack of money. He took a job selling advertising space, and was almost immediately successful. Within a few months he was making very good money.

Then came the dilemma. The money from his job allowed him to live well and to travel. It gave him leisure time to enjoy a variety of diversions. The medical degree would require time in night school and years of sacrifice. Then there would be the long process of building a practice.

Another increase in his income led him, after a long struggle, to decide to forgo medical school. Will he be a success at what he does? Probably. Will he ever be satisfied at work? Probably not.

Be slow to give up your dream.

Having assessed your possibilities, is there any reason success should elude you in a country as alive with opportunity as ours is?

To achieve your long-term purpose, you may have to stay with your old job while you prepare yourself for the new. If you are married, your spouse may have to work full or part time for a while. You may have to economize, postpone a major purchase or a vacation.

In the end, you may decide to stay with what you are now doing and commit yourself to doing it better.

This in itself would be a gain.

Still can't make up your mind whether to go or stay? You might try an old-fashioned but useful device. Draw a line down the center of a sheet of paper and write PRO and CON at the top.

List on one side the reasons you should change jobs and on the other the reasons you should not.

Take care not to weight your responses — this is no time for self-delusion. Take as much as a week to work on your list. Consult your spouse or a trusted friend. Your friend may not understand all the ramifications of your problem, may not be equipped to give you the advice you need and may not have the best judgment, but the act of spelling out the dilemma and the available options will help you to see the situation more clearly and often in a new light.

The act of verbalizing a problem helps to clarify it.

You might ask: Shouldn't I consider my employers in this? If I am going to leave their employ, what are my obligations to them?

I have always believed that an employee's obligation to an employer is simply to give the company his or her best.

Have no illusions about business loyalty. There are exceptions, of course, but your employer will be loyal to you only so long as he benefits from your work. That is reasonable and just. Their primary obligation is to the company. A company is not a charitable organization, and if you are no longer making a positive contribution to it, the company is doing a judicious and not a callous thing in letting you go.

You do owe your employer one thing: reasonable notice of your intention to resign.

Look first, then leap

It is time now to make your decision and, having made it, to act. Don't postpone your decision until you have all the facts — you never will have all the facts, and if you are not resolute you will find yourself suffering from what has been described as "the paralysis of analysis."

If the decision is to change your job, what's next?

Begin by systematically surveying your options. You are planning a life-shaping decision, so don't be precipitate. Scrutinize your proposed vocation from four standpoints:

- Will it be work you will be challenged by and will enjoy? Or may you, after a few years, find yourself as bored and dissatisfied as you are now?
- Does it hold a potential sufficient to satisfy your ambitions not merely for the moment but for the years ahead?
- Will it provide the income you want, not simply what you need but what you would like to have?
- Is it in a field that has a future or one that is in danger of becoming outmoded?

Answer these questions first. Don't jump from the frying pan into another frying pan.

If you are married, discuss the move with your spouse. But the opposition of a wife or husband is not a sufficient reason to cause you to draw back. No partner in a marriage should, out of an undue concern for security, saddle the other with a lifetime of frustration.

Begin to make inquiries. Talk to friends. Seek introductions. Mail out job applications — erring on the side of too many rather than too few.

Now, face to face with the reality that changing jobs isn't necessarily going to be the exciting adventure you may have thought it might be, don't grow discouraged. Remind yourself that you have embarked in this direction because you were at a dead end.

Above all else, remember this: You are changing vocations to change the remainder of your life.

Look at the future with your eyes wide open. Accept the fact that it may take you months, even years, to get established in a new field. But keep at the forefront of your mind the thought that, from this point on, you will be doing what you want to do. The zest you bring to work you enjoy almost guarantees success.

In the meantime, what's the worst that could happen to you?

You may go through a few trying months — nothing measured against a lifetime — but if you have exhibited the courage and determination voluntarily to opt for a new direction in life, you won't stay down long. At few times in history has it been easier to make the leap of faith than it is today.

A personal experience

What qualifies me to advise you on a career change?

At age forty-one I found myself faced with beginning life over again. I was living in New York City and working for the Presbyterian Church, responsible for the denomination's outreach program. During the previous four years I had been travelling from coast to coast in the United States and Canada, speaking to tens of thousands nightly. For three years I had also hosted the weekly program, *Look Up and Live*, on the CBS television network.

But I was losing my faith.

I had entered the ministry as a fervent youth of nineteen, but now I found myself doubting the essential tenets of Christian belief. Much against my will — for I very much wanted to believe — my mind had begun to challenge and finally to rebut the things I believed. Finally, I decided that I must leave the ministry.

It seemed that all of life had been turned on its end. My mother was dying of cancer, a shell of herself at the end of a prolonged illness. I was cutting myself off from virtually all of my friends. I was abandoning the men and women I had influenced to go to the mission fields and into the ministry. I felt like a betrayer.

But I had no real choice. I couldn't stay in the ministry, paper over my doubts and daily live a lie. I packed my few possessions in a rented automobile trailer and started on the road to Toronto.

It was an intimidating time. How would I earn a living? What was I fitted for? Who would hire a forty-one-year-old former preacher?

I decided to try to write. Living alone in a two-room cottage on Georgian Bay, I wrote three television plays, which I sold to the Canadian Broadcasting Corporation.

A producer who had seen me on CBS hired me as co-host of a new CBC public-affairs television series he was producing, and my feet were set on a new road.

So, if after mature consideration you are convinced that you should move to another field or to another job, stop contemplating it and act. Don't let the prospect oppress you; rejoice in it. Let it be the adventure it is. Pay heed to qualified advice but disregard the nay-sayers. Franklin Roosevelt was right: The only thing to fear is fear itself.

And focus on the advantages you have.

I have an acquaintance who came to Canada from Holland some ten years ago. He had no relatives in North America. He knew only a dozen words in English. Everything he owned was in two suitcases and a steamer trunk. Today he is a certified public accountant, has a large staff working for him and owns a commodious home and a vacation condominium in Florida. In the meantime he has married and has three children.

Your situation is undoubtedly better than his was. Many of you were born in this country. You have friends and relatives here. You are fluent in English or French. You are familiar with the world of commerce. You are certainly no confused stranger in a strange land.

But even if you are an immigrant, look about you. Observe how many newcomers have come to this land and have moved up the ladder to success.

You can, too.

So don't wait to awaken some morning when you're seventy to ask yourself, "Why didn't I do that thing I wanted so much to do? Why did I let myself be deterred? Why, at least, didn't I try?"

> For of all sad words of tongue or pen,
> The saddest are these: "It might have been!"

FOR REVIEW

(1) Half our waking hours are spent at work. To permit half of your conscious life to be wasted in some disliked drudgery is to act the fool.

(2) Most of those who want to change their vocation but fail to, do so because of fear and inertia.

(3) A change in the pattern of life takes an act of will. You will stay where you are unless you summon your resolve, persevere in your determination and act.

(4) Before moving to another job, determine whether you resent authority and are better suited to going into business for yourself.

(5) Before you commit yourself to another career, assure yourself that it has the potential to challenge and reward you through a lifetime.

(6) If you find yourself stymied by "the paralysis of analysis," remember this: You are changing vocations in order to change the remainder of your life.

5 | How to Make Yourself Needed

BUSINESS EXISTS TO MEET NEEDS, whether those needs are for a service or for a product. But businesses themselves have needs, and their primary need is for competent, creative people.

Therein lies opportunity. Make yourself needed.

Go beyond that and make yourself indispensable and there is no limit to the success you may achieve.

The single greatest need of any senior executive is for a competent and imaginative staff: men and women who will help him reach his goals.

The head of any company, whether it is General Motors or a boondocks widget manufacturer, knows that he will succeed or fail, expand or end in bankruptcy, to the degree that the company is able to recruit competent and creative men and women.

He knows that, among the people working for him, there are the imaginative and the dullards, the ambitious and the indolent, the diligent and the time servers. His hope is that, among these, there will be some who can stand with him, help him to meet his responsibilities, assist him in achieving his goals. Perhaps even make unique contributions.

If he is a wise employer, he is ever on the lookout for such people.

He may institute an in-house program designed to discover and develop the latent talent on his staff. He may turn to a headhunting organization in the hope that it can bring him the right candidates. However he may go about it, he knows he cannot do the job alone and that he needs to draw to himself men and women who will contribute to what he hopes will be the escalating success of the company.

And there you are — anxious to succeed.

The question is: What can you do to make yourself needed?

Perceiving a need

The world of commerce is based on meeting needs. Someone needs a product or a service and someone supplies it. For all its great variety, that is what business is about. One organization's need encounters another's supply, and the two of them do business. It is true of automakers and motorists, lawyers and clients, baseball teams and fans, prostitutes and johns.

So understood, the secret of success is simple: Find a need, supply it, and you will prosper.

Unfortunately, it is difficult to perceive a need. Yet when someone does just that, and meets the need, it often seems so obvious that you almost involuntarily exclaim, "Why didn't *I* think of that?"

A case in point: Not many years ago, when men and women wanted to dine out, they went to a restaurant. They had many options, of course — restaurants came in an infinite variety. And they were usually pleasant places. The food was fancier than home cooking, and prices were tailored to the ability to pay.

The need seemed perfectly met.

But there were disadvantages, especially for those in a hurry or those who had children or those who had to watch their expenditures.

To eat in a restaurant, you had to make a reservation, and despite that, sometimes wait to be seated. The menu offered so many choices it was difficult to decide. It was hard to catch the waiter's eye. Often the food came from a steam table. Frequently, there was little on the menu that appealed to the kids. And, more often than not, you flinched when you got the bill — especially after you added the mandatory ten to fifteen percent tip.

Thousands of men and women in the restaurant business were aware of the need. One of them, an entrepreneur by the name of Ray Kroc, decided to meet it.

In the mid-1950s he chanced to stop at a drive-in restaurant in California run by two brothers, Dick and Mac McDonald. Intrigued by their approach to the marketing of fast food, he made a deal with them, and after much thought opened a new kind of restaurant in Des Plaines, Illinois, under the now famous golden arches.

Ray Kroc's restaurant would be unlike the usual eating place in almost every way. No reservation would be needed. There would be little or no waiting. There would be no *maître d'*. The choices would be limited to the most universally popular selections. Everything would be grade-A quality and would be freshly prepared. There would be no linen or cutlery or flowers on the table. And, of fundamental importance, the food would appeal to children.

By getting rid of printed menus and waiters and steam tables, tablecloths and cutlery — even salt and pepper shakers — and by moving customers out quickly, Kroc cut his costs, increased his volume and was able to offer fresh, tasty food for one-half to one-third of the price charged by the average restaurant. And there were no tips.

Kroc pioneered the fast-food industry, and in the process, by franchising his idea and letting smaller entrepreneurs in on it, he became very wealthy.

He saw a need and he met it.

The company you work for may seem to be meeting the needs of its customers, but is it?

The management of the company may be so burdened by keeping abreast of the competition that it barely has time to meet current needs, much less perceive new ones.

The personnel of your company may be so occupied with internal problems — cash flow, difficulties with suppliers, internecine rivalries, lack of innovation and planning, general indifference or boredom — that many of the people who buy your products or services are becoming restive.

In this hypothetical situation, in which so many needs are not being met, what can you do?

And where should you begin?

Knowing your business

Begin by setting out to learn precisely what it is your company does, and how it does it.

Your response may be: "But I know what the company does — we make and sell lamp shades. Some models are manufactured in our plant and others are imported. We've been in business forty-two years and we distribute our products in department stores and lighting-fixture stores in the United States and Canada."

Good. But do you know in how many of the fifty states and in how many of the ten Canadian provinces? And if you do not sell in all the states and provinces, why not? Why do you make only lamp shades and not lamps? Why are some of your products manufactured in the plant while some are imported? How are new products developed? Do you have a busy season and periods when production and sales slacken? What are the reasons for these fluctuations? Are sales increasing or are they static — even slipping? Who are your strongest competitors? Which is the dominant company in the field? Precisely why is it more successful than you are? What are the most frequent complaints from your retailers and your customers? Are there patterns there?

If you don't know the answers to these and other questions, you don't really know what your company does. And if you are serious about being useful to your employer, you need to know not only the questions but some of the answers.

In a word: You need to know your business. If you don't know your business, you will thrash about aimlessly and in confusion and finally give up because you are going nowhere.

Knowing how your business operates

It is not enough to know about the product or the service your business markets. You need to know something about the day-to-day operation of the company.

- What continuing problems does the company have in its internal operation?
- What procedures frequently develop glitches?
- Is there good communication between the various levels of management and between management and staff?
- Is there much dissatisfaction among the employees?
- Is it standard me-against-the-company bitching or is much of it legitimate?
- What practices are outdated?
- What procedures are redundant?
- Where is there a waste of money or time?
- What is the most frequent customer complaint?

Learn everything about the business you can. Only by being aware of the company's needs can you contribute to meeting them. The more you contribute, the more you will make yourself needed.

Some words of caution: Seek to learn about your company by observation and by judicious questioning, not by sticking your nose into other people's business and becoming a meddlesome busybody. Begin in your own department. Clean up your own backyard. Be sure, before looking beyond it, that you are meeting your own responsibilities fully and imaginatively.

When you perceive a problem in some other department, don't sound off about it. It is easy to see needs; it is difficult to meet them.

Put your head down and think.

And don't be presumptuous. Don't assume that other people aren't aware of the problem and aren't concerned about it — you weren't until yesterday. They may not be, of course, and your scrutiny of the problems might reveal that. But you will make a serious mistake if you presume that wisdom was born with you.

If you isolate a problem of consequence, begin to think about what can be done to resolve it.

If the problem is costing the company money or good will, go to the person to whom you report. Write a brief, informal report. Draw your boss's attention to the problem and suggest what might be done to correct it. Conclude by saying something as simple as, "Thought you'd like to know."

Go over the boss's head and you may make an enemy. Give the information to the boss in a positive manner and you will have made a friend.

It is not difficult to improve the operation of any organization, but it is by no means easy. Useful innovations are usually the product of persistent thought.

Don't settle for easy solutions.

The secret of monetary success

The best-paid men and women in the business world are those who make themselves needed. They don't get rewarded simply for hard work — ditchdiggers work hard and their pay is a pittance. What is valued is not hard work; it is *creative* hard work. When you give to your job not just your time and your muscle but your brain, your contribution and the subsequent rewards can escalate.

Think for a moment. Who are the best-paid people in business? They are people who, by their talents or their actions or their judgment, have made themselves essential to a company's success.

When Lee Iacocca left Ford, why was Chrysler willing to pay him a king's ransom in salary and bonuses? Because he had the managerial skills and the daring Chrysler needed to remain solvent.

Why are baseball players like Dave Winfield, George Brett, Don Mattingly or José Canseco paid more than a million dollars to play a game for only six months of the year? Because by exhibiting their skills they are able to drive in runs and bring in the fans.

Why is Bill Cosby the best-paid television entertainer in the world? Because millions of people want to watch him perform, and TV networks and advertisers need audiences such as his to stay in business.

Could a lesson be more obvious? *Do something that will help a business to make more money and the business will gladly pay you a portion of that money to work for it.*

Manufacture a product or perform a service that a lot of people will pay money to obtain (I'm not sure a better mousetrap will do it any more) and your company will declare a dividend.

The secret of success is to make yourself needed.

Perceiving problems

In seeking to devise or improve a product, a service, a procedure or a system you are moving into the realm in which an inventor works. (For a more detailed look at how the inventor/innovator works, see Chapter 7, "How to Become an Innovator.")

The inventor or innovator begins by perceiving a need. If you are hoping to solve problems by coming up with new or better ways to do things, you should understand the basics about the creative process.

Go back to one of the earliest innovators, the genius who invented the wheel.

How did he begin? He began by perceiving a problem: the problem for which the wheel was the solution. He knew intuitively that before you can solve a problem you must understand it. The problem was this: If you wanted to move something too heavy to carry — a boulder, say — you had to manhandle it until it was resting on the ends of two long poles lying on the ground and lashed together. Then you could seize the poles at the opposite end and pull. Optionally, you could harness horses or oxen and have them pull.

But the system was unsatisfactory. The friction was great. The ends of the poles dug into the ground and dragged debris with them as they skidded.

The Inventor puzzled over the problem, realized that he needed to lessen the friction involved and eventually came up with the wheel. In the wheel, the friction is transferred from the ground to the center of the axis where it is less and great loads can be moved easily.

Be warned: It is not easy to solve problems that require innovation. You will need persistence, determination and creativity. Depending on the degree of difficulty, you may not find the solution in days or weeks.

But it is there to be found. Puzzle over it. Make notes. Dissect the problem so you are fully aware of its nature. Ponder it while driving to work. Discuss it with your spouse or a friend. Think about it last thing at night. The problem won't give up its solution easily. Be heartened, though: problems do get solved — but only if you put your mind to the task and persist. And having persisted, persist.

Teamwork works

With your mind set on working your way up in the company structure, let me make an unorthodox suggestion. Look for an ally.

Observe the people around you. Look for the person — ideally someone at your own level — who is clearly bent on going somewhere in the company. It will be a person who is ambitious, committed and given to hard work.

Form an alliance with that person.

First, get to know him — or her, as the case may be. Look for interests in common. Observe him carefully, seeking to determine if your personalities might mesh.

Satisfied that he is bright, trustworthy, ambitious, invite him to lunch and make your proposal. Point out that you seem to have many things in common, not least your jobs. Say you would like to join forces. Tell him you would like to set aside a time each week in which to share ideas about the business, to test those ideas in discussion and finally to present them to management.

Meet your associate each week for lunch or at home — anywhere convenient — and bounce ideas off each other. You will find that two heads are better than one, and that each of you can supplement and improve the other's ideas. Then translate your ideas into action.

Don't try to dominate the relationship, but don't be dominated. You need each other. And don't be clandestine about your meetings; it's not a conspiracy, it's creative teamwork.

You will need a way to transmit your ideas and suggestions to management. It should be done in such a fashion as to make it clear that the material is the product of your collaboration.

It is imperative that you put forward your comments in such a way as not to create jealousy or enmity among your fellow-workers or immediate superiors. Put your suggestions in writing and offer to discuss them further if desired.

You will probably find that your ideas are welcomed. If they are good ideas, they will enable your superiors to look good. Don't resent it if you or your friend don't get all the credit due; you are making yourself needed. Be assured that, if your suggestions are useful, your superior will not want to offend or alienate you. Even if you don't get full credit, your actions can do you nothing but good.

Above all, do not seek surreptitiously to spread the word that the new system being installed or the change in personnel relationships just instituted is your idea. Let the credit go to the person who got the changes made. Undermine your boss and you undo all the good you have accomplished.

Will you encounter jealousy or resentment? That will depend a great deal on how you handle yourself. Try to anticipate such problems. If they become serious, you have two minds to deal with the dilemma — yours and your friend's — and that will make it easier.

Don't be aggressive. Don't be smart-ass. Don't tell yourself that you and your associate are God's gift to business. Avoid an us-versus-the-system mentality.

It is possible that your associate will be praised or moved up the ladder and you won't be. This may happen to either of you for a variety of reasons. Despite any initial disappointment you may feel, be happy about it; you are a team. If your friend is advanced, he is in a position to help you. If you are advanced, you will help your friend.

It could be a relationship that will carry both of you all the way to the top.

Look for no more from the joint venture than a chance to contribute to the company and thus enhance your position. You are making yourself needed. If the alliance is a good one, the attention and the rewards will come in their own time. If it isn't, you can each go your own way no worse for the experience. But determine to make it work.

The most important part of the arrangement is, of course, choosing the other person. The chances of achieving compatibility are probably no better than fifty-fifty. So take time and particular care to make the right choice. Making that judgment wisely will be a demonstration of your potential managerial ability.

Seizing an opportunity

You can make yourself needed by a company even before you work for it. Here is an example.

A man I hardly knew telephoned late one evening to seek advice. He was fifty-four, a middle-management executive, experienced in the hardware business. He had lost his job when the company he was working for failed. He was having great difficulty finding another. In his search he had discovered that his age was a disadvantage, and he was growing desperate. In ten days he had an appointment with the president of a hardware chain, and he was deeply concerned. Another rejection might mean the beginning of a gloomy future.

What could he do to make the best impression?

Obviously, the challenge was to make the president see that he needed him. But how? I suggested that in the intervening ten days he commit himself to learn what problems the company had at the retail level. He could study the company's outlets in his city. He could look for problems, play customer, see what irked or pleased him about the products or the service. I told him to list the products or services lacking in the store and to note whether the stock was well displayed. Were there delays at the checkout counter? How might the process be speeded up? Was it difficult to find things — a drill bit, for instance, or a telephone jack or a piece of glass cut to a particular size? Was the store layout ideal? Were specials or bargains highly visible? Men like to browse in hardware stores; what incentives were offered to encourage them to do so and, as a consequence, to make impulse purchases?

I told my friend to give the matter concentrated thought over the next ten days, to work at it night and day. Then to list his suggestions in a an organized presentation and leave the list with the president at the end of the interview.

In a word, I said, convince him that he needs you and that you will be worth more than he will have to pay you.

The interview proved to be a near disaster. The session was interrupted three times by telephone calls. It became obvious that there was some kind of internal crisis, and the president seemed distracted. There were apologies, but the interview was cut short. My friend left in despair.

Three days later he was hired. His demeanor during the interview, but mostly the specific proposals he had left behind, had convinced the president that he needed him.

Make yourself needed.

FOR REVIEW

(1) Business exists to meet needs. But businesses themselves have needs, and their primary need is for competent, creative people.

(2) The best-paid people in business are those who make themselves needed. The secret of success is simple: Find a need and supply it.

(3) Begin by learning precisely what your company does and how it does it. Only then can you perceive what its needs are.

(4) It is not easy to solve problems that require innovation. It will take persistence, creativity and determination.

(5) If you are determined to make your way upward in the corporate structure, find an ally.

(6) It is possible to make yourself needed by a company even before you work for it.

6 | Learning to Make the Right Decisions

I WILL TELL YOU what the single most valuable skill in business is.

It is not raw talent.

It is not skill with words.

It is not sales ability.

It is not a head for figures.

It is not managerial know-how.

The single most valuable skill in business, the ability for which companies are prepared to pay large sums of money, the attribute that makes an employee indispensable and that guarantees success, is good judgment.

It is the ability to make the right decisions most of the time.

Why is this skill so valuable? It is because a corporate structure is essentially a decision-making apparatus.

The objective of a business is to sell a product or a service. Its ultimate success depends not only on the quality of the product or service offered, but also on the quality of the decisions made by the people who run the business.

Make enough bad decisions and you are out of business. Make enough good decisions and you will prosper.

Successful corporations prosper because they are well run. More specifically, because they are well run at the top. The chief executive officer is more important than the board of directors, more important than vice-presidents, more important than managers and employees.

It may justly be said that the CEO is as important as what the company sells. For unless the product is continually upgraded and properly merchandised, unless there is diversification in the wares offered and constant adaptation to changes in the marketplace, the company will go down the drain.

Do you sometimes gasp with astonishment when you read of the enormous salaries — not to speak of the stock options and other perks — paid to the heads of large corporations? Is anyone worth that much money?

The answer, in many cases, is an unequivocal yes. They are worth every dime of it. These men and women are paid princely sums, because they contribute more than any other person or thing to the success of the companies they head.

They have developed the ability to make difficult decisions, decisions from which major consequences flow, and to be right most of the time.

One of the reasons these people manage to make good decisions most of the time is that they have troubled to develop a staff with decision-making ability to work with them.

The wise CEO knows that problems flow upward, and that if a problem is of major consequence, it will end up on his or her desk.

He also knows that if he spends most of his time resolving problems, he will not have enough time to deal properly with his other responsibilities. So, because his time and energy are limited and the demands on him are many, he finds ways to delegate some of his decision-making responsibilities.

The person to whom the responsibility is passed must be trusted to take judicious action, or the original problem will be compounded and the CEO will then have to deal with the original problem plus the additional problems created by the failure of his delegate.

Herein lies the value to a corporation of men and women at any level who have developed the ability to make good decisions.

Acquire that skill and your journey up the corporate ladder is assured.

Can decision-making be learned?

There are people who seem by nature more skilled at decision-making than others. The likelihood is, however, that the ability is not innate but that it was acquired in the early years of childhood.

Some parents do everything for their children, spoil them, as the phrase has it, and the children find it unnecessary to work things out on their own. Other children learn by doing. "Put away your toys," they are told. "Tie your shoelaces. Put the blocks in the matching holes."

The child who is required to work things out — with loving help, of course — begins to realize that things don't simply happen. Certain things happen only because certain other things happened first.

Surely that is the principle learned when a child is taught to tie shoelaces: "If you don't make the knot before you make the bow it won't work." One accomplishment makes another possible. If you make something work and you are praised for it, you feel good and begin to realize that you will be rewarded for doing things well.

In the process of figuring out how things work, you learn that sometimes a decision can make things work. In placing the shapes in corresponding holes, children learn that, if they fit the round and rectangular pieces first, the rest are easier. They learn that actions have consequences and that, by figuring out what actions are required, they can achieve the desired consequences.

Later, life authenticates these lessons.

Children who have everything done for them don't learn how to make decisions — the decisions are made for them. Not having acquired that know-how early on, they tend to be indecisive throughout life.

So, while it may appear that good judgment is intuitive, it is really an acquired skill. And, in accordance with the principle that skills tend to improve with use, we enhance our ability to decide as we mature.

Maybe you find it easy to make decisions or maybe you struggle to come down on one side or another; it doesn't matter. The point is: You can learn to if you want to, but only if you are prepared to work at it.

Two types of judgment

There are two types of judgment: the snap judgment and the considered judgment. The difference between them can be seen clearly in the experiences of two groups of people whose life's work is the making of decisions.

One is a fight judge. He sits at ringside making a considered decision as to which of two boxers is the victor.

The second is a baseball umpire. He stands behind the catcher making a snap decision on each pitch.

What are the differences in the mental processes in each case?

In boxing, the action takes place during three-minute rounds with one minute between each round. Points may be scored through offence and defence, by aggressiveness, by initiative, by punishment inflicted or by "controlling" the action. Moreover, partisans cheer each punch by a favorite and their bias can be intimidating.

A boxing judge must weigh all these factors, accord them their relative importance, discount the partisanship of the crowd, dismiss personal feelings about each fighter and make a considered judgment.

The umpire's task is equally difficult but entirely different. To be called a strike, a pitch must pass through an imaginary rectangle directly above the plate, called the "strike zone." A simple enough task if the ball travels in a straight line; but it doesn't. It curves to the left or to the right, or it falls away. The ball may travel at ninety-five miles an hour or lob in at half that speed. A pitch may be within the strike zone when it is a foot in front of the plate, or when it lodges in the catcher's glove, but not as it passes the batter. Add to that the fact that everyone in the stands is ready to second-guess the call.

With all this complexity, how is the umpire able to make a decision, and make it without a moment's hesitation?

First, the umpire analyzes the basic facts. He knows that some pitches will clearly be in the strike zone and some far out of it. No problem — a child could call them correctly. He knows also that most pitches will be on the edges of the invisible rectangle and thus in question. He knows further that the ball passes through the strike zone in a split second. Consequently, he will have no time for deliberation. His calls must be conditioned reflexes. The totality of the impressions entering his brain must trip a physical action — the calling of a ball or a strike.

The umpire does what must always be done when someone makes a snap judgment: he lets the input trigger a programmed response. He does not weigh the various factors; he responds to a stimulus on the basis of experience.

The boxing judge has a very different task. He must weigh all the information transmitted to his brain during the various three-minute periods, factor in other considerations and come to a conclusion.

The judge makes a considered judgment — he acts.

The umpire makes a snap judgment — he reacts.

The snap judgment

A minority of business decisions are snap judgments. Indeed, as a general rule it is wise to avoid them. Because a snap judgment is essentially a reflex action — all the revelant factors cannot be fully evaluated — there is a strong possibility of error. Some people pride themselves that they work best under pressure, and delight in making snap judgments, but it can be a costly conceit. Decisions made on the spur of the moment can have consequences that reach far into the future and may be long regretted.

But although few business decisions are snap judgments, occasions do arise when immediate decisions are necessary. How is it possible to do better in making such quick decisions than you would by simply flipping a coin?

It is a matter of preparing the mind.

The major-league umpire is experienced. He has done his apprenticeship in the minors. He has been tested in the fire and knows his business. So, when a certain sequence of events happens during the delivery of a pitch, he has "been there before." He is familiar with a similar set of circumstances. He doesn't need to review all the facts; they are lodged in his experience. In a sense, his snap judgments are considered decisions.

The situation is similar in business. The man who has immersed himself in his business, who knows it inside out and has taken pains to stay abreast of change, is equipped to make snap judgments and will, more often than not, make wise ones.

Nonetheless, unless there is no option, it is usually the better part of wisdom, having made an instant decision of consequence, to add the rider: "Let's sleep on it."

The considered decision

Considered decisions are the bedrock of business success — your company's and your own. You will live or die by them. Make good decisions most of the time and you will get ahead. Make poor decisions and you will languish in the ruck.

The obvious counsel for those who would improve their ability to make wise decisions is this: "First, get the facts."

The advice is of little value, however, unless it is followed by the admonition: Get all the facts, both the hard and the soft.

The hard facts are usually obvious. They have to do with recorded experience, with dollars, with the results of research, with plant capacity, with market data and other specific information.

They are objective. They are measurable. You can put them on paper or enter them into a computer and make sense of them.

But there are other facts: unsubstantial, unpredictable, personal, uncontrollable. They are not subject to precise measurement. You can't spell them out or enter them in a computer.

They are the soft facts, the "what if?" facts:

•What if there is a downturn in the economy?
•What if Williams isn't the person to handle it?

•What if the competition gets the jump on us?
•What if our offshore source of supply is cut off?
•What if the union won't renew its contract and walks out?
•What if the market forecasts are wrong?
•What if the financing doesn't come through?

These and other imponderables are among the soft facts that must be considered before a decision is made.

There is a temptation to grow impatient with such questions and override them. ("There are no answers to those questions, dammit! Let's get the show on the road.")

But, in any project, the "what if?" factors are often the things that spell success or failure. To fail to examine them closely is to court trouble.

It is not that "what if?" questions are unanswerable; it is simply that they are not subject to black-and-white answers. They can be evaluated. Conclusions can be made as to the likelihood of one result or another. It isn't a crapshoot; it's more of the nature of odds-making.

The response to a "what if?" question is not, "Let's flip a coin," it is, "Let's do the necessary digging and see what kind of answers we can come up with. We're not going to get black-and-white answers, but let's not settle for anything less than a fully informed judgment."

The criticism might be made: "That's not decision-making; it's temporizing." No, it's decision-making. You have made an interim decision to get all the available facts before you make your final decision.

Anything less wouldn't be decisiveness; it would be foolhardiness.

The perils of indecision

Now to the techniques.

The first step is to realize that decisions must be made; they cannot forever be postponed. Too often, in facing a tough decision, the matter is left unresolved in the unspoken hope that "things will work out." But there comes a time in any examination of a problem when the facts are before you and further discussion will only confuse.

At that point, muster your resolution and commit yourself.

The failure to make a decision is itself a decision — it is a decision to postpone. You must make the decision or your indecision will make the decision. Procrastination is often more fraught with peril than is an imperfect decision.

Realize also that indecision feeds on itself. The act of postponing compounds your confusion and makes the ultimate decision more difficult.

Getting good advice

In working toward a decision of consequence, use the talents of your associates. The dictionary defines the word "decision" as "a determination made after consideration or consultation." It is foolish to train a staff and then to disregard the contribution it can make.

The cliché "It's lonely at the top" is used to describe the isolation of the man or woman who bears final responsibility for the decisions made in a business, decisions on which the success of the organization may depend. But it is a mistake to impose that isolation on oneself.

Some senior officials don't talk to their juniors; some do all the talking. There are many so-called consultations that waste the time of everyone involved. The chairman delivers himself of his view, and having done so, continues to do most of the talking: dominating, brooking few interruptions, maundering on.

On such occasions one is sorely tempted to say: "Look. You know what you know and we know what you know; why don't you now pay some attention to what the other person knows?"

No one wastes as much time as the man with the massive ego who gathers his associates and then does all the talking. He is not open to new ideas — wisdom was born with him. His greatest mistake is that he deprives himself of the help available to him.

We need each other — at every level.

A fable is told of a man who visited hell. There he saw millions of men and women, emaciated and starving. The astonishing fact was that they were seated at a great banqueting table, the table groaning under the weight of every kind of food and drink. They were starving because, although every individual had a great spoon attached to each forearm, the handles of the spoons were so long that when they filled them they could not bring them to their mouths.

In the fable the man was then transported to heaven. There, too, he saw millions of people at great banqueting tables, all with similar spoons attached to their forearms. But these people were well fed and happy. Why? Because they were feeding each other.

We depend on each other.

There are many heads of corporations who permit themselves to become isolated. Such isolation is unwise and can be disastrous.

If the top is seen as the peak of a pyramid, there is room for only one and it is a lonely place. But if it is seen as the top floor of a building, where associates are at hand for discussion and counsel, the decision-making responsibility becomes less onerous and more efficient.

The greatest mistake a manager or supervisor can make is to become isolated from his subordinates. The men and women who report to him are the nervous system of the organism. The messages they communicate reveal the health of the corporate body. To disregard their contributions, to fail to establish a system for channeling their knowledge is, sooner or later, to become out of touch and uninformed.

How imperative it is then that the autocratic boss or the arbitrary manager or supervisor establish a means by which frequent readings on what is happening in the body corporate can be channeled upward. And how important it is frequently to consult, to learn to listen, in the realization that the views of others can enhance or alter your own views — even reveal their flaws.

The stages in decision-making

There are four stages in the making of decisions:

(1) Get the facts (information)
(2) Get help (consultation)
(3) Get on with it (action)
(4) Get past it (conclusion).

You cannot deal with a problem, much less resolve it, if you don't know precisely what the problem is. This is made more difficult by the fact that it is very easy to misread a given situation.

For example:

- What appears to be the failure of a product may be the failure of a marketing strategy.
- A series of staff problems may stem, not from a company policy but from the arbitrary way that policy is being administered.
- A running feud between two of your senior people may not be the result of differing approaches but of personal antipathies.
- An ineffective advertising campaign may not be the fault of the people devising it but of your failure to provide clear guidelines.

So the first step in dealing with a problem is to ascertain what the problem is.

The president of a major television network had a problem. He had suffered for the better part of year from severe headaches, periods of dizziness and fainting. He had seen a series of doctors — in desperation, even flying to another city to see the acknowledged expert in the field. But none of the doctors could diagnose the problem. Each time the man underwent a physical examination on a doctor's table, the symptoms would disappear.

One day he faced a minor emergency. He was scheduled to attend an important dinner meeting and needed a clean shirt. There wasn't time to return home, so he slipped out of the office to a nearby haberdashery. When the clerk asked him his size, he told him, "Sixteen. At least I think it is. I've worn only custom-made shirts for years and I'm not sure."

The clerk looked at him, bemused. "Impossible. You're at least a seventeen. Here, let me measure you."

The fellow had put on some weight and had been wearing shirts a full size too small. When this was remedied, his symptoms disappeared.

Because he had not identified the problem, all the efforts to solve it had been in vain.

Don't solve others' problems

Before you deal with any problem, try to determine whether it should have come to your desk in the first place.

It may be something that a subordinate should have dealt with but, ducking ultimate responsibility — a not uncommon tendency — has passed to you.

Duly noted, pass it back. There is no surer way to reduce your effectiveness than by spending your time solving other people's problems.

If the problem is one you should handle, it is often useful to pass it to one or two others. Ask them to do three things: to analyze the problem, to present possible approaches and, finally, to propose a solution.

The procedure has three advantages. It helps your own analysis, by providing the benefit of other minds; it provides insights into the abilities of the people you ask; and it may serve to separate the merely competent from the talented.

The procedure will also enable you to instruct your staff in the decision-making process by analyzing with them your own eventual determination.

Four types of problems

Four types of problems come to the decision-maker's desk, and each requires a different approach.

First, there are the nonproblems, temporary difficulties that are better left alone. Get heavy-handed in dealing with them and they may develop into real problems, or you may be perceived by those who work with you as a fussbudget.

Second, there are the incipient problems. They are there but their shape is unclear. Note their existence, and check on them regularly. In this way you will be able to deal with them before they become serious.

Third, there are the immediate problems. These are by far the largest in number, and they should be dealt with immediately. With your experience and training, most of them can be taken care of without lengthy consideration or consultation. Such problems are the stuff of daily decision-making.

Fourth, there are the fundamental problems. These are dilemmas relating to the basics of your business:

- With the product or service.
- With the defection of a senior member of your staff to a competitor.
- With the failure of a major supplier.
- With the need to change procedures within the company.
- With an aggressive new challenge from a foreign competitor.
- With an opportunity to expand.
- With the appearance of a new product or technique that outdates some of your products.
- With a sudden market vulnerability.

The fundamental problems separate the mediocre managers from the movers and shakers. They can make or break a company; they can lead to labor peace or prolonged turmoil; they can end in disaster or a round of congratulations from your superiors.

The fundamental problems take time to resolve. And when they arise, time must be taken.

Sufficient time.

Priority time.

Other problems must be made secondary. Counsel must be sought. Studies, if needed, must be begun. Subsidiary responsibilities must be delegated.

Incidentally, in the matter of delegating — delegate!

In the office of the founder and long-time president of the Toronto Star, J.B. Atkinson, there was only one wall decoration. It was behind his desk and thus visible to any member of the staff meeting with him. It read:

HOW TO MAKE A DECISION
(1) Decide what needs to be done
(2) Delegate the authority to do it
(3) SEE THAT IT IS DONE

When you delegate a responsibility, take your hands off. Get the problem off your desk, and go on to other things. Require progress reports, of course — not to do so is to court disaster — but don't keep looking over that person's shoulder. Nothing will so inhibit your delegate and waste your time.

The only job from which I resigned in frustration and anger was as editor-in-chief of *Maclean's* magazine, known as Canada's national magazine. I was hired with promises of an increase in income, a leased luxury automobile and other perks. As well, I was given a new and spacious office and offered a fully paid-up pension.

But soon there was trouble in Paradise.

The vice president to whom I reported could not keep his hands off my job. From my first day, I received frequent memos from him with comments, criticisms and story ideas, most of them worthless. Every day I received four, five, sometimes six instructions or pointed suggestions. There was constant interference. I answered all the memoranda at first, then some of them and, after a few weeks, none of them. Within three months we had reached an impasse.

There came a showdown in his office. I said, "Everywhere I have worked I have operated under one rule: If I am doing my job well, leave me alone. If I am doing it poorly, fire me. I cannot work with someone peering over my shoulder and second guessing my every move. Please get off my back."

There was no change, and I resigned three months later.

A senior executive who delegates a responsibility and then meddles is wasting time and talent. The premise behind the delegation of authority is that, by so doing, the senior executive is free to do the more important tasks.

The actions of a manager-meddler are very much like those of the mother-in-law who cannot release her son and continues to intrude in his married life, ruining it.

Once a task has been delegated, the senior official should retain only two concerns: to insure that the task is done and to receive regular reports on the progress being made.

Analyzing problems

In dealing with a fundamental problem it is imperative, first, to be certain that you understand precisely what the problem is. Before moving to solve it, you must perceive it clearly. Make sure you know what to focus on.

If you don't know what the problem is you can't resolve it.

It is a useful discipline to put the problem in writing: in a brief statement that can be encompassed within, at most, a single sheet of paper, ideally, in a single paragraph.

If a problem is amorphous, little can be done to solve it. It is like "trying to nail jelly to a wall."

It is essential to ascertain the essence of a problem because what may have been presented to you as the facts may be little more than opinions, and opinions are often colored by personal attitudes or perceptions.

There is a tendency in all of us to think that our view of a given situation is the right one. This is why we often preface our assertions by saying, "The way I see it is . . . "

But with problems of consequence, there is usually no "correct" way.

Indeed, even when a solution is found, it will not necessarily be the right one — it will more likely be the best of the available options.

In diagnosing a serious problem in medicine, it is often helpful to get a second opinion. And in diagnosing your problem in business, it may be judicious to get more than one view of it and of its solution.

The pro and con method

If your problem is a relatively simple Yes or No quandary, you may wish to consider an old but useful procedure, one advocated two hundred years ago by Benjamin Franklin:

When confronted with two courses of action, I jot down on a piece of paper all the arguments in favor of each one. Then, on the opposite side, I write down all the arguments, pro and con, canceling them out, one against the other. I then take the course indicated by what remains.

His system may be useful in some circumstances, but in others it may be inapplicable; mostly because there are usually more than two courses of action available. The principal reason for listing the options available and their advantages or disadvantages is to keep the problem and its various aspects clearly before you. The act of making a list assists in your analysis.

Having made your list, draw a line across the bottom of the paper and note those factors that have to do not with concrete facts but with the "emotional" aspects of the problem, with the personalities involved or other intangibles.

The isolation of these intangible factors will often cast light on and suggest solutions to the conflicts that arise out of the hard data.

Simple problems may not need a complex analysis, but major problems do. One of the difficulties in dealing with a complex problem in your head is that you may get too many balls in the air and, in the resulting confusion, forget some facts or become mesmerized by others.

With the problem clearly delineated, ponder it. Sleep on it. If you have friends with business sense, talk it over with them. Because they have no personal involvement in the situation and no preconceptions their counsel may be more valid than an associate's. (One caution: Don't tell them your view when you are asking for help. They might, out of misguided friendship, be disposed to concur.)

Misleading "facts"

In dealing with problems, you may be tempted to give undue weight to the opinions of your money-people. As they will tell you, they deal with facts, not opinions, with the irrefutable logic and orderliness of balance sheets, with the realities that come out of a computer.

But it is a fatal mistake, in making a decision, to give the greatest weight to the opinions of the accountants and financial experts. There is a false mystique about accountants and scientists and pollsters and such — that emotion has no part in their thinking, that they deal solely with facts.

This is, of course, nonsense. Their "facts" are, in part, opinions. Statistical facts without interpretation may be misleading and are not automatically to be trusted.

Here are two statistical facts. Both are true, but both are misleading.

Statistical Fact One: The leading cause of death in teenagers is suicide. Statistical Fact Two: Most automobile accidents happen within eight miles of home.

It is a sobering thought that the leading cause of death in teenagers is suicide — until you remember that disproportionately few teenagers die from other causes.

It is a sobering thought that most automobile accidents happen within eight miles of home — until you remember that ninety percent of driving is done within eight miles of home.

The two statistics are both hard facts. But taken out of context by themselves they are misleading. So it is with many other statistical facts: they are useful only when they are set alongside other facts.

Accountants and money people live with statistics and numerical facts, and the service they render is unique and invaluable. But their contribution to any decision-making process must be seen for what it is: one of many factors to be considered.

In the 1950s, the Ford Motor Company was facing serious financial problems. Company accountants came to the board of directors, grimly set out in tables of figures how grievous the problems were and argued that, to remain solvent, the company must shut down two plants. The advice was taken.

Not long afterward, the accountants again came before the board, presented their fiscal arguments and recommended further closings. The gloom and indecision were broken when John Beasley, a veteran member of the board, interjected, "Wait a minute. Why don't we close down the entire company? That way we'll *really* save money."

Actuarially, the accountants' advice was sound. But it was not the only counsel to be reckoned with. In the end, other voices prevailed and the company went on to a period of increasing expansion.

Money people tend to be conservative — and such voices are needed to counter the high rollers — but theirs are not necessarily the most important voices.

In the making of any corporate decision, financial counsel must be recognized for what it is: data to be disregarded at your peril, but not necessarily the most important data.

The role of the computer

We tend today to be unduly impressed by the data in a computer printout.

The computer, undoubtedly one of the half-dozen most useful inventions in history, is a magnificent and tireless servant, a genie capable of Brobdingnagian tasks. At lightning speed it can ingest disparate and complex information and bring order out of chaos.

Because the computer is so versatile, so swift and so tireless, we tend to invest it with an authority that is not due it.

A computer is simply a superior abacus. It is capable of doing two things — arithmetic and sorting. It astonishes by its performance, but it answers only questions that a person can ask, and it can only make conclusions with the data it has been fed.

It can do nothing a person can't do. The significant difference is, of course, that it does in seconds what might take one person a dozen lifetimes.

It is a convenience. An adjunct. A tool. But no more.

We think of a computer as logical, but of course it isn't; it is a mechanism. It will provide answers as brilliant or as fallible as the person using it. Input fact and you will get fact. Input error and you will get error — although the computer will sometimes draw the error to your attention.

You can best understand its limitations if you compare a computer with a human mind.

You would never say of a computer, for instance, that it is profound. Nor would you describe it with such words as astute, rational, perceptive, reasonable, sane, intelligent, sober, wise, probing, insightful, brilliant, reflective, studious, discerning, discriminating or subtle.

These are qualities of the human mind, qualities that are of paramount importance in the making of wise decisions. They are not within the scope of any computer program.

If you want to develop good judgment, you will have to do your own thinking. You can draw upon the advice of others and the logic and incredible capacity of a computer, but you must finally use your brain.

There is no option.

Thinking is hard work, and there are many who take great pains to avoid it. But, there is no escaping the fact that concentrated thinking, more than anything else, is the basis of good decisions.

FOR REVIEW

(1) The single most valuable skill in business is good judgment, the ability to make the right decisions most of the time. Good judgment is an acquired skill and can be learned.

(2) There are two kinds of decisions: the snap judgment, in which the individual reacts, from experience, and the considered judgment, in which the individual acts on information.

(3) Decisions must be made; they cannot forever be postponed. The failure to make a decision is itself a decision — a decision to postpone.

(4) Executives who make major decisions alone deprive themselves of information and of the collective wisdom of their associates.

(5) There are four types of problems: nonproblems, incipient problems, immediate problems and fundamental problems.

(6) There are four stages in making a decision: Get the facts (information); get help (consultation); get on with it (action); get past it (conclusion).

(7) No major problem can be solved until it has been analyzed. If you don't know what the problem is you can't solve it.

7 | How to Become an Innovator

I HAVE A FRIEND who earns a very good living as an inventor. He works, not in the research division of a great corporation where elaborate technical facilities are available, where skilled associates can be drawn into the quest for a solution to a problem, but by himself in a small workshop with nothing but the requisite tools at hand.

He defines his job as problem-solving. He views it as perceiving needs and then supplying them. His goal is to meet needs by creating something that never existed before.

I think of him as an explorer, a descendant of that storied man who observed that there was an abundance of mice and then built a better mousetrap. Whereupon, the story goes, the world beat a path to his door.

These things my friend is. The one thing he is not is a dreamer.

He doesn't waste his time vaguely hoping that one of these days he will, by some happenstance, stumble upon an idea that will bring him fame and make him rich. He defines his goals, then sets out to reach them.

He makes a lot of money by being inventive.

If you hope to be successful in solving your problems and meeting your needs, you are going to have to learn to be an inventor.

Perceiving needs

You may feel more comfortable about the possibilities if I use a different word: "innovator."

"But," you say, "innovation is impossible for me. That's not the way my mind works. I don't have that knack. I'm good with figures. I'm a proven salesman. I'm an efficient executive and I have leadership qualities. I can do lots of things but I am not a creative thinker."

Nonsense.

I am convinced that, with very few exceptions, anyone can be creative. And I am not alone in this opinion. A respected Massachusetts teacher, George Prince, is the founder of a consulting firm called Synectics. Giant American corporations such as Chase Manhattan Bank, IBM, Gillette, Digital Equipment and Wang Laboratories send members of their staff to Synectics to learn the techniques of creativity. George Prince spends his life communicating the idea that anyone can be creative.

We tend to believe that inventiveness — or creativity, imaginative thinking or whatever else it may be called — is a rare gift. It is true, there are a few extraordinarily gifted people, some who approach genius. It is also true that there are millions of less gifted individuals who nonetheless have fertile imaginations and inventive minds and latent talents that only need developing.

How to begin? Let me return to my inventor friend. He begins by perceiving a need. And anyone with two eyes and two wits can do that.

We perceive needs every day of our lives. Something doesn't work — that's a need. The trouble is that most of us don't see it as a need; we see it as an inconvenience. And rather than do something about it, we curse it: "The damn thing doesn't work!"

What is required is not a flash of irritation, but a solution.

Which brings me to the second function of the inventor. He

doesn't only invent things, he fixes things that don't work. Or he makes things work better.

That is precisely what the innovator in business does. As does the inventor, the business innovator begins by perceiving a need.

- A system in your office doesn't work. That's a need.
- Consumers don't realize that your product is superior to the competition's. That's a need.
- The brochure describing your company's services isn't clearly written. That's a need.
- There's an abnormal amount of bitching among the staff. That's a need.
- There's a rumor that your principal competitor is about to launch a much improved model of their product. That's a need.
- The weekly staff meeting is a waste of time and a bore. That's a need.

All these are needs crying out for solutions.

You may think you're not creative, but pause to ask yourself: Are you really incapable of perceiving the needs at your place of work? And if you see them, do you really lack the talent to come up with solutions?

Perhaps you *can* be an innovator.

The challenge in a problem

Innovators have a special attitude toward life. They are born tinkerers. When they see something that doesn't work, their immediate inclination is to fix it.

They believe there is a better way to do anything. And they are right.

Most of us are not like that. We follow established procedures like sheep; because they are there. Even if the procedures are faulty it would never occur to us to question them, much less try to change them. Why?

- Because that's the way it has always been done.
- Because the boss wants it done this way.
- Because I haven't got the time to think about changing it.

95

So we live with the problem and there it remains, and probably will remain until someone comes along who isn't satisfied with simply perceiving problems but wants to solve them.

Every problem raises two questions:

(1) What makes it a problem?
(2) How can it be solved?

It isn't difficult to spot problems; some of them remind you of their presence every hour of every day. Moreover, there is usually someone in the organization who feels called upon to draw them to everyone's attention. He or she is the office griper:

"That damn water fountain doesn't produce more than a dribble."

"The mailboy never puts the interdepartmental mail on the right desk."

"The handle on this damn filing cabinet falls off at least once a week."

"Why doesn't somebody do something about the phonelines; I keep getting calls that should go to Sales."

It would never occur to the office malcontent to tell Maintenance about the water fountain or to have a friendly chat with the mailboy. It is easy to criticize; it takes thought and effort to change things. Which is precisely why innovators — the great and the ordinary — are valuable to a corporation. They make it run better.

How can you develop your creative skills?

Begin by asking yourself: "How can I do what I do better than I am doing it?" As you keep asking, you will begin to see problems not as problems but as situations asking to be solved. That will start you thinking.

"Necessity is the mother of invention" is a truism because needs breed solutions.

Innovation isn't easy

Having perceived a need, how does the innovator proceed? This is the unglamorous part of innovating — the hard work.

By far the largest part of an inventor's days are spent in coming up with solutions that don't work. They try this, then that, and having tried everything they can think of, they persevere.

That's the name of the game: trial and error.

In a familiar story, Thomas Alva Edison perceived the need for a source of illumination better than gaslight. He told friend about the numerous setbacks he had encountered in trying to solve the problem.

The friend commented: "Then you have failed 283 times."

"No," Edison replied. "I now know there are 283 ways that *won't* work." He persisted until he found a way that would, and the incandescent light was created.

Understand before you begin: For all the zeal you may bring to a problem of consequence, you are not going to solve the problem with a wish and a snap of your fingers.

Solutions to real problems don't come easily. If they did, someone would have come up with them. If the problem you are puzzling over could be solved in an hour, it wouldn't be much of a problem. And the reward for solving it wouldn't be much, either.

As you approach a problem, hold this at the forefront of your mind: One of these days someone is going to solve it. If it is a problem of consequence, the person who solves it will have taken a step up the ladder of success. Problem-solvers are usually well rewarded. The reason: They benefit the company.

Resolve to be that person.

Persistence pays

Let this be understood: I am not suggesting that anyone can solve any problem.

If you are tone-deaf you are not likely to detect a discord in a symphony. If you have flat feet you are not likely to become the world's best high jumper. And if there is a problem in trigonometry, don't look to me! Although we are all capable of far more than we think, we are all less gifted in some areas than in others.

So play to your strengths.

Innovating is like fishing. First you survey the area, looking for the place with the most promise. Then you check the wind to insure that when you drop the anchor you will drift into the exact spot chosen. Next you select the ideal lure for the kind of fish you hope to catch. Then, you check your reel, and cast.

And cast.

And continue to cast until you get a strike — even if it takes most of the morning.

Innovating works somewhat like fishing. You are after an elusive, invisible prize. You may not have success where you are casting. After giving it a good try, you may have to move to another area. You may want to try an unorthodox bait. The fishing may not be good on this particular day at this particular time; and you may have to come back tomorrow.

That's what you do when you're fishing.

And that's what innovators do. They persist.

Harnessing the subconscious

How can you harness your subconscious mind for problem-solving and creative thinking? The first step:

(1) Determine precisely what the problem is.
If you don't know what you're looking for, you won't find it.

Spend as much time as necessary to define exactly what the problem is. You need a target so you can focus your thoughts. Narrow the problem down so you can state it in a sentence. Write out the sentence, and then examine it.

Is it an exact statement of the problem or is it a generalization? If it is vague, refine it until you state in one succinct sentence exactly what the need is.

Am I overstating the necessity of determining what the problem is? No. When you go to the doctor for treatment and he asks you where it hurts, it isn't enough to say, "Well, sort of here and there." Before he can treat you he needs to know exactly where the problem lies.

John Dewey, the great American educator, said, "A problem well stated is half solved."

(2) Having defined the problem, analyze it:

- What are its components?
- How long has it existed?
- Who is involved?
- Is it a people problem or a technical problem?
- Is it a matter of consequence or merely an irritant?
- What are its manifestations?
- Who is responsible for it?
- Will you be stepping on toes if you take it on?
- Are there reasons it hasn't been dealt with?
- Do you contribute to it?
- Should you consult someone about it before proceeding?
- What will happen if you resolve it?
- Is it only part of a larger problem?

(3) Allocate time to finding a solution.

By time I don't mean an hour — it might take days. Puzzle over it. Ponder it. Badger your brain. Think about it while driving to work. Consult others. If there is written material on the subject, read it. Make it a point to think about it just before falling asleep. Having exhausted the rational approaches to the problem, think far-out; go questing beyond the standard parameters. Live it, eat it, sleep it, dream it.

Then, after you have exhausted all the available possibilities, forget about it.

Yes, forget about it. If you have given it your best effort, your subconscious mind will come up with a solution.

At some point in the following days — almost certainly within two to three weeks — suddenly, without warning, a solution will break upon your consciousness. It may come in that moment between sleep and awakening, while you are in the midst of a conversation, while you are busy, while you are cleaning your fingernails or pulling on your left sock or walking the dog — but it will come. Your subconscious mind, that part of the brain that never sleeps, has continued to ponder the problem twenty-four hours a day; analyzing the data, appraising it, collating it and, finally, making it cohere.

You are familiar with the expression, "Eureka! I have found it!" It was uttered by Archimedes the Greek physicist-inventor when he suddenly came up with the solution to a complex problem he had been puzzling over for an extended period of time. You may find some similar exclamation coming to your lips when, as the result of your commitment to the resolution of a problem, the answer suddenly comes.

Haven't you already had the experience? Worried about something, persistently seeking a way out of a stubborn dilemma, suddenly, during an off-guard moment, when the matter is far from your mind, your imagination has surprised you with a solution.

Or to use a more familiar example: In a heated discussion you are exasperated when a familiar word or a name won't come forward. Then, suddenly, while driving home, out of nowhere, the word pops into your mind. But it *didn't* come from nowhere: your subconscious mind had continued to look for the word, and having come up with it, presented it.

I make the promise that the technique will work for you because I have used it again and again and have over the years developed a quiet confidence that it will not fail.

The subconscious at work

In January 1985, I watched an extraordinary scene during a television news show. Some forty men and women were seated around tables heaped with tens of thousands of crumpled dollar bills. They were straightening them out and stacking them in piles.

The reporter explained that the money was part of one day's receipts on the streetcars and subway trains of the Toronto Transit Commission. Each day, seventy-five to one hundred thousand individual dollar bills were dropped into the fare-boxes and there was no option but to count them by hand. The volume of bills was expected to increase in 1986 to thirty-six million.

My mind fastened on the need. I puzzled over it for days. Surely the cumbersome process could be mechanized. But how? No two bills were folded alike. Some were wadded or crumpled into balls. Some of the bills were crisp and new, others were pliant and worn.

Each had to be straightened out and arranged face-up in packets of fifty to be accepted at the bank.

How could the problem be solved?

Two weeks later, as I awoke, a thought sent me leaping from the bed. In great excitement, I dug into my wallet and into my wife's purse, gathered all the paper currency we had, folded the bills into every configuration, twisted some and squeezed still others into crumpled pellets. Then I filled the kitchen sink with warm water and immersed them. My subconscious mind had reminded me that many fabricated materials had a "memory," a tendency to return to the shape that had been impressed on them.

I held my breath. As I watched, each of the bills slowly unfolded. I was able to seize them by an end and withdraw them to the palm of my other hand, flat and face up. The rate of retrieval by the TTC staff was 8.3 bills per minute; without difficulty I was able to stack more than thirty.

I moved to patent the system and presented it (including a simple method for drying the bills) to the TTC. They welcomed it and built the necessary mechanical apparatus. (Typical of the inventor's lot, the one-dollar Loon coin was introduced and the TTC put the process on hold.)

I do not assert that, using the technique, you will necessarily come up with the only possible answer or the best answer to a given problem. But at the very least, it will clarify the problem and help you deal with it.

Raymond C. Johnson, in his exceptional book, *The Achievers*, draws attention to some relevant words from the American patriot, Alexander Hamilton, one of the more extraordinary of those extraordinary men who fashioned the American republic during the latter part of the eighteenth century. Here is his answer when asked how he had gone about making his singular contribution:

"Men give me credit for some genius. All the genius I have lies in this: When I have a subject in hand, I study it profoundly. Day and night it is before me. My mind is pervaded with it. Then the effort which I have made results in what people are pleased to call 'the fruit of genius.' It is actually the fruit of labor and thought."

FOR REVIEW

(1) When innovators see something that doesn't work, their immediate inclination is to fix it. Innovators believe there is a better way to do anything. And they are right!

(2) Innovators begin by perceiving a need and seeking to do something about meeting it. It takes no special talent to see needs and no great talent to solve them. It does take persistence and imagination.

(3) Every problem raises two questions: Why is it a problem? How can it be solved?

(4) The way to begin to develop creative skills is to ask yourself: "How can I do what I do better than I am doing it?"

(5) The surest way to success and exceptional rewards is to become an innovator. The ability is not rare, and it can be learned.

(6) Learn to harness your subconscious mind; it is a great problem-solver.

8 | The Art of Communicating

THE ONE BASIC SKILL without which you cannot possibly succeed in business is the ability to communicate.

You may have the finest brain since Einstein's and the greatest ideas in history, but unless you can get the ideas out of your head into other people's heads you will not succeed.

Why? Simply because, no matter how good your ideas may be, unless you communicate them to others they remain yours and yours alone. For your thoughts to be useful they must be imparted to someone else.

Nothing in human relations is as fundamentally important as communicating.

Every day of our lives we seek to communicate different things: ideas, opinions, hopes, feelings, needs. Do it well and life is richer, more rewarding, less complicated. Do it poorly and our days are filled with misunderstandings, frustration, wasted time, explanations and alienation.

Communicate poorly in business and you are likely to be a failure, or at least to come short of your potential. Learn to communicate skillfully and you are well started on the road to success.

Most of the time in an office is spent communicating: Send a memorandum to the staff; you're communicating. Dictate a letter; you're communicating. Talk to a client on the telephone; you're communicating. Report to the boss on a project; you're communicating. Prepare a press release; you're communicating. Reprimand a secretary; you're communicating. Report to a board meeting; you're communicating.

The ability to communicate skillfully can enhance your effectiveness and a corresponding inability can doom you to mediocrity.

How well do *you* communicate?

You can answer by asking yourself a few simple questions:

- Do you frequently find yourself being misunderstood?
- Do you often say things you don't mean or fail to say what you do mean?
- Do you catch yourself saying: "What I'm trying to say is ... "?
- Do you often say, "That's not what I meant; I meant thus and so"?
- When you sit down to write an important letter or memorandum, do you struggle to get your ideas on paper?

The inability to communicate effectively is a major handicap in your quest for success. It means you get off the mark slowly, get delayed along the way and fall behind in the race.

It is a serious problem in personal relations, but it is fatal in business, and if you hope to get ahead you dare not let it continue.

The inability to communicate

This and the next three chapters examine ways by which you may improve your communication skills, your vocabulary, your ability to write or speak well. But, as background, let's go back to fundamentals and get a clear understanding of what communicating is.

We live in what might be described as the age of communication. Never in history has there been so much information and so many ways by which it may be shared. Information can be passed from person to person by the spoken and the written word. It can be disseminated by radio, television and print, by computer and facsimile networking and in dozens of other ways. Yet, for all these advances it is entirely possible that there have been few periods in history in which we have communicated so poorly.

The problem is this: We mistakenly assume that whenever we speak or write, we are communicating.

No assumption could be more mistaken.

EXAMPLE: Nearly half the marriages in North America end in divorce. Talk to divorced people about what went wrong and one complaint you will invariably hear is this: "We just couldn't *communicate* with each other."

It wasn't that they didn't talk — they talked a great deal, endlessly it sometimes seemed, often with great heat, frequently far into the night.

But for all the talk they were unable to communicate.

EXAMPLE: We are all familiar with the term "the generation gap." It was coined to describe the gulf between people of one generation and the next — more specifically, between parents and children. The term signifies that between people of different generations there is often a great chasm across which it is difficult to communicate.

The term is certainly applicable today. Ask the father having trouble with a son what the problem is and he is likely to reply with some exasperation, "You just can't talk to that kid!" Question the youngster and he will say, "My dad and I don't speak the same language."

But of course they do. They speak the same language but they don't *communicate*.

EXAMPLE: The same problem is evident in politics. As it has been from the dawn of time, the world is divided into armed camps. It is true of the Communist world and the democracies; it is evident in the Americas, the Middle East, in Africa, in the Orient. Decade after decade, nations have exchanged threats, glowered over fortifications, reheated cold wars and from time to time triggered their earthquakes.

The problem is not that each side doesn't make its views known — the air is filled with propaganda. But there is little communication.

A similar situation obtains within nations; between people of different backgrounds, different incomes or different colors; between liberals and conservatives in politics; between unions and management in business; between tenants and landlords in daily life. Even between the sexes. You can see it on the streets and in the courts, read about it in the newspapers and watch the disputes on television. Enmities. Quarrels. Polarized opinions. And usually because we fail to understand each other.

Why such frequent and persistent conflicts? It is in large part because we don't understand how to communicate.

Transmitting ideas

What is communication? *It is the process by which you get an idea from one head into another.*

Communication began with a need: the need to share an idea. Early man didn't have language; he communicated with grunts and shrugs and gestures. But such non-verbal communication was limited to the transmitting of only the simplest ideas. So man began to experiment with a variety of grunts, using them to identify things.

For instance: Someone in prehistory may have pointed at a canine and grunted "dog." After this was done a few times, the friend would catch the meaning, and repeat the sound. As a consequence, when next they wanted to refer to the dog, it didn't need to be present. There was tacit agreement: the sound "dog" signified a canine and the grunt had become a word.

It is interesting to note in passing that even today the elementary words remain monosyllabic grunts. For example: I, me, you, he, she, go, come, stay, eat, fight, kill, die. Grunts like these in a primitive language enabled men and women to transmit ideas from one head to another.

To communicate.

Over the centuries these primitive exchanges were refined and grew complex, and it became possible for men and women to communicate complicated and sophisticated ideas.

As language evolved, however, it became evident that, for all the acquired fluency, the listener didn't necessarily hear what the speaker intended. Why? One reason is that words have subjective meanings, personal and emotional overtones.

EXAMPLE: I speak the word "love" before an audience and ask them to contemplate it for a moment. I am thinking one thing, but each member of of the audience is thinking of something different.

Love. A child thinks of her mother, a youth his beloved, a bride her groom, a patriot his country, a religious her God, a romantic his dream. The simple four-letter word "love" conveys something different to each individual who hears it, each conception being determined by the total of that individual's experiences with love.

So it is with many words, words such as pride, sex, friendship, beauty, honesty. Words connote different things to different people.

Our reaction to them is largely emotional.

Beyond that, words take on overtones depending on who speaks them. In the words of the aphorism: "What you are speaks so loudly that I can't hear what you say."

Two politicians, one a liberal and the other a conservative, speak to an audience about private enterprise. Hearing them, you will automatically filter through your own biases the presumed biases of each speaker. As the expression so aptly puts it: "You know where he's coming from."

Who we are colors what we say — and, equally important, what is heard. If you wish to communicate effectively you will have to bear in mind the roadblocks in other people's minds, roadblocks such as prejudice, acculturation, biases, wariness or apathy. With these and many other hindrances to mutual understanding it is little wonder we communicate as poorly as we do.

Getting inside the other person's skin

So what is the remedy?

The path to effective communication is to attempt to hear through the other person's ears, to get inside the other person's skin. It is to so identify with that person that you are sensitive, not only to what you are saying, but to what the other person is hearing.

The great communicators hear what they are saying through their listeners' ears.

Communication is a dialogue. As you speak you must constantly be aware of the impressions forming in the mind of your listener.

The skilled advertising writer is not writing to please himself but to interest the consumer. Successful politicians take pains to tell their constituents what they know they want to hear. The effective insurance salesperson introduces no subject that does not relate to the prospective client's fears or desire for security.

They speak to people where they are.

The problem for most of us is that we are so caught up in what we are saying that we pay little attention to what is being heard. Unfortunately, what is being said and what is being heard are often two very different things.

There is an injunction: "Don't just stand there; say something." The effective communicator inverts it so that it goes, "Don't just say something; stand there." Stand where? In the other person's skin. Your concern should be to so relate to your listeners that your concern is not merely what you are saying, but what they are hearing.

There is nothing novel in this; we do it all the time.

When we speak to a child we simplify our speech. Conversing with someone not fluent in English, we articulate clearly and choose our words carefully. We know that, if we want to be understood, we must do this.

I am not proposing that you talk down to others. In fact, nothing could more effectively block what you are trying to communicate than the impression that you feel yourself above your listener. What must be done is to so identify with your audience that you hear what they hear.

And equally important, what they feel.

Try this as an exercise, then make it a practice. The next time you have the task of winning someone to your view — an employee, a client, a spouse, a son, a daughter or a friend — think through what you want to say. Then sit down with an empty chair opposite. Imagine that person in the chair and make your pitch.

Then get out of your chair and sit where the other person would sit. Repeat your arguments. But this time, listen to them as though they are being directed at you, you being the other person. You may find that your words take on very different overtones and are not nearly as convincing as you thought they were.

Ask yourself: "Would my points convince me if I were the other person, if I were doing the listening rather than the talking?"

You may find that what sounds convincing in the speaking is very different in the hearing.

Communication is a dialogue

Whenever you seek to persuade another person to do something, you engage in a dialogue. As you make your points, questions or opposed views will arise in the mind of your listener. Unless you are aware of this and ready to deal with it, you are likely to encounter disagreement.

You have your opinions and objectives; so does your listener. It is not enough simply to speak your mind; you must, even as you make your arguments, be sensitive to the questions or the objections your words are stimulating. If you cannot sufficiently empathize with your listener to understand this and to counter these objections as you go, you will end your conversation divided.

Hearing what you are saying through the other person's ears is called diplomacy. It is also essential to the engineering of consent.

This is not to suggest that you waste time rebutting unasked questions — it was said of one politician that "he was always answering questions nobody was asking." It is to suggest that you approach any discussion in which you are trying to change someone's mind with an acute awareness of what is being heard.

You cannot be an effective communicator unless you have a feeling for people. If your objective is only to get others to do what you want them to do, they will know it and will react negatively.

No one can influence anyone unless a bond of sorts is formed. A connection must be made. You need to be on the same wavelength. There must be a rapport that can best be described as trust.

What makes an effective communicator? It is not simply the result of verbal skills. The impact of an extraordinary communicator — a Winston Churchill or a Franklin D. Roosevelt — is often described as mysterious, but it is not. It is something that derives from that individual's essential self.

Ronald Reagan was called "the great communicator." Despite the fact that his inattention to detail was well known, that his concentration span was short, that he presided over rather than ran his administration, he was able to go to the people at crucial times and win a majority to his views. Why? Because, even if people disagreed with his politics and viewed him as a bumbler, they liked him. Something coming from the man engaged their interest and their trust.

It was said of Ronald Reagan that he understood the medium of television and knew how to use it and that this was the reason for his impact. But television is filled with slick communicators: attractive people whose words are crisply articulated, whose voices are perfectly modulated and who never fluff a line. The television industry describes them as "projecting sincerity." But we recognize them for what they are. They are people employed by others, mouthing words they never wrote, presenting ideas they don't give a damn about. They are hirelings.

Why do we react so adversely to the fast-buck salesman? It is because we know he has one interest: his own. He is trying to use us and we resent it. There are tens of thousands of salespeople who never make that second sale. They may be hotshots in the initial presentation but they are duds on the follow-up. There is no mystery to it: their concern is only for themselves.

Communicating isn't simply a matter of saying something well, it has to do with the essence of the person saying it. You.

Don't manipulate, motivate

In trying to win other people's assent, remember that the goal is not to manipulate but to motivate. Try to manipulate people and you will eventually arouse hostility. Motivate them and you will add their enthusiasm to your own.

Adolf Hitler manipulated the German people by appealing to the postwar resentments they were feeling and to their fear of Communism. He used his extraordinary oratorical skills to weld his compatriots into a war machine that ravaged Europe and kindled fires around the world.

Winston Churchill understood the roots of British pride and resolution and used that knowledge to motivate his countrymen and prepare them for the Nazi buzz-bombs and the razing of London.

The ability to engineer assent is a valuable skill; it is also subject to abuse. If you know how to sway others' opinions you may be tempted to use the ability to your own advantage. In the long run, it doesn't pay. Business is based on the mutual advantage of the buyer and the seller. Take all the chips and soon you will have no one to play with.

What is the difference between manipulating and motivating? Manipulation is an attempt to use people. Motivating is seeking to be of use to people. Use people and you will eventually lose them — as employees or customers or friends. Motivate them and you will both benefit.

In 1953 a letter came to the National Council of Churches in the USA from the ministerial association of Richmond, Virginia, inviting me to conduct a two-week preaching mission in that city. Richmond is a lovely, cultivated city. During the American Civil War it was the capital of the Confederacy. I accepted the invitation, making mention that the meetings would have to be unsegregated.

"Sorry," I was told, "the city bylaws forbid racially integrated public meetings." After an extended exchange of correspondence, the city council set aside the prohibition for this one occasion.

On the opening night of the campaign the tension in the auditorium was palpable. Very few blacks arrived; those who did, unsure of the situation, sat in the balcony. I called the head usher backstage. "Don't just hand out songbooks," I said. "Usher the people to their seats. Downstairs and in the balcony. White and black."

But the battle was not yet won. Few blacks attended. After decades of segregation they were not prepared automatically to accept this temporary concession. I asked for a meeting of all the black clergy and their senior officials and specified that the press be barred. They filled the auditorium of one of the larger African Methodist churches.

I spoke bluntly. I reminded them that we had fought to have an integrated campaign and that a historic first had been achieved. "But now," I said, "after years of being segregated because of your color you are doing the same thing to the whites. That's your right. If you are free to attend, you are free to stay away. But in doing so, realize that you are perpetuating a system you hate."

I decided to tell them a story about Mohandas Gandhi, the great Indian civil rights leader. Addressing a meeting of blacks in South Africa, Gandhi had said, "One of our problems as colored people is that we act as though we were a minority. The fact is that the colored peoples of the world are a majority. When we use the terms 'colored' and 'whites' we demonstrate inferiority feelings. We should speak instead of colored people and colorless people."

The church rocked with shouts of "Amen." When silence returned, I said, "As a member of a minority group — the colorless people of the world — I want to plead with you to cooperate with me in this campaign."

There was an immediate increase in the number of blacks at the meetings. They sat in every part of the auditorium, sang in the choir and worked as ushers. In the two weeks of the campaign there was not a single untoward incident.

Had the black citizens of Richmond been manipulated or had they been motivated? Yes, their attendance helped serve one of my purposes — to gather great crowds of people — but an infinitely more important end had been achieved: the meetings were the first public demonstration south of the Mason-Dixon line of the peaceful integration of whites and blacks in a public assembly.

The line between manipulation and motivation is not always clear. Having learned how to achieve assent, some will be tempted to use this knowlege to exploit others. There are temporary advantages to be gained in doing so, of course, but more often than not these benefits are short-term and finally self-defeating.

The Harvard Business Review lists the ability to communicate as "the most promotable quality anyone in business can possess." Fortunately, it is a skill that can be learned. Not to take the time and effort necessary to become a good communicator is to make unlikely your business success and to limit yourself in every relationship in life.

FOR REVIEW

(1) The basic skill without which you cannot hope to succeed in business is the ability to communicate.

(2) Most of the time in any office is spent in communicating. The failure to do so skillfully is to doom yourself to mediocrity.

(3) Communicating is the process by which you get an idea from one head into another. The effective communicator attempts to hear through the other person's ears, to get inside the other person's skin.

(4) Communication is a dialogue. As you speak you need to be aware of the impressions forming in the mind of the listener.

(5) In trying to engineer assent, remember that the goal is not to manipulate but to motivate.

9 | Communicating on Your Feet

THERE ARE FEW SKILLS more valuable than the ability to say precisely what you want to say, whether to an individual or a group, and few areas of special competence that will serve you better than being able to speak effectively in public.

Despite this, few people master the art of public speaking. Most speeches are boring, the speaker's eyes fixed on his manuscript rather than on the audience, the high point being the words, "And now, in conclusion . . ."

An occasional speaker can bring an audience to its feet with a flight of oratory, but that is exceptional. Most standing ovations are prompted by the rising to their feet of a few front-row partisans, the remainder of the audience following grudgingly.

What is surprising is that there are so few good public speakers when there are millions of men and women who are good talkers. *Public speaking is little more than a specialized form of talking,* and anyone who is a good conversationalist has the potential to be a good public speaker.

The reason so few people are good on their feet is that they have false notions about what effective public speech is.

They mistakenly believe that the style used by most politicians and preachers is the requisite model and they seek to imitate it.

There was a time when the cadenced speech of the politician and the sonorous tones of the ecclesiastic were acceptable, but no longer. The effective speaker of today simply talks to the audience. Granted, it is a specialized kind of talking, but essentially it is the normal expression of your thoughts with some adjustment for the fact that the occasion is large and your audience is more than a few.

The old patterns were born of necessity. There were no sound systems to amplify the voice, and speakers had no option but to shout. Today, such is the quality of the sound systems, even a whisper can be clearly heard in the back row of a stadium seating one hundred thousand.

A majority of men and women in business learn to converse with ease and to write with competence, but few learn to speak well in public.

If this is true of you, you are limiting your potential, for people who can sway an audience, whether that audience numbers a few or many, have an enormous advantage over their fellows and will, inevitably, be given opportunities that are not offered to others.

The secret of public speaking

But let's get down to specifics. How does one learn to think on one's feet and become an effective public speaker?

I have been speaking from public platforms for fifty years, to audiences of fifty to fifty thousand. The question most asked of me following these occasions (apart from those related to the subject matter of the address) is this: "How can I become a good public speaker?"

I invariably give the same answer. I say: "If I were a concert pianist would you ask, 'How do I become an accomplished pianist?' No, you would know the answer without asking: Go practice your scales. And if you ask how you may become a good public speaker the answer is the same: Practice."

There is no other way.

Good enough, you say, but how does one practice public speaking? Am I to search for audiences on which to inflict myself? Am I to stand on a street corner and rail at the passersby?

Of course not. You begin by training your subconscious mind.

In the performance of grand opera there is, at floor level, hidden from the audience at the front of the stage, a person called a prompter. The prompter's job is, when necessary, to remind the artist of the words to the aria she is singing.

The subconscious mind (sometimes called the unconscious mind) is our prompter when we speak.

You will understand this better if you realize that in everyday conversation you do not consciously choose words and form sentences; most of that is done by your subconscious mind, unbidden.

We sometimes say, "You know, I didn't have to think; the words just came." And they did. Even as you spoke, your subconscious mind was rummaging about at lightning speed in the memory bank of your brain and supplying the words as you needed them.

This happens every time you speak.

You don't consciously form the proper syntax. You don't say to yourself while in a conversation, "I must be sure, now, to have a subject and an object in each sentence, as well as the proper form of my verbs." You don't charge yourself while chatting with someone, "Be careful to use the past tense and not split your infinitives or you will seem like a fool."

Of course you don't.

If while talking we had consciously to obey all the rules of grammar and select from the thesaurus of the mind the appropriate words, we would stammer and stumble.

There is, of course, no need to do this. From that moment in childhood when we uttered our first words, we have been training the subconscious mind to do it for us, automatically. The conscious mind remains free to think about the ideas, the facts and the impressions we want to communicate. Our servant, the subconscious mind, does the legwork.

You can understand how this works if you think of what happens when you express yourself in a language in which you are not fluent. Because you are concentrating on finding the appropriate words and using the right tense, each sentence is a struggle. In a language such as French you must also concern yourself with selecting the proper gender for your nouns. Little wonder the learner stumbles.

It is no problem for the French, of course. They learned the gender of their nouns while they were learning to talk; it is all lodged in their subconscious.

How marvelous that, when you speak in your mother tongue, the computer you have been programming from childhood is at work in the brain, selecting the words you require and fashioning them into coherent sentences!

Talking under pressure

I dealt specifically with training the subconscious in Chapter 1, "The Winning Edge." Let me confine myself here to the use of this faculty in public speaking, when the mind is distracted by the unfamiliar circumstances and our thought processes are slowed by self-consciousness.

Here is an exercise which, practiced assiduously, will make you as fluent before an audience as you are in a one-on-one conversation with a friend.

For a few minutes each day, do this: Select any object in your field of vision — the view from a window, a passerby on the street, a bookcase, a picture on the wall, a dog before the fireplace, anything — and talk about it non-stop for thirty seconds. The object need have no significance; it need only be in your line of sight.

The important thing is to talk about it, without pausing, for a minimum of thirty seconds.

Having begun, don't stop. Even if what you are saying becomes gibberish, keep going. Talk about the object's color, its function, its surroundings, its contours, its parts, its uses. If you run out of things to say, repeat yourself. Don't strive to be clever or even coherent; concentrate on persevering until the thirty seconds is up.

The benefits you will derive from doing this exercise are phenomenal.

Why? Because you are training your subconscious mind to work under pressure. You are requiring it to come up with specific words, to form intelligible sentences without considered thought, to function without conscious direction, despite distractions.

The exercise is hard work, and you may find it difficult. For the first few days your sentences may be awkward and stumbling. But that will quickly change.

If you stimulate your body, exercise it, challenge it, it will increase in power and capability. So it is with the brain. Mental fitness can be acquired and the thought processes made more effective.

The rule applies equally to your mind and your body: Use it or it deteriorates.

Learning to talk on your feet

Let us turn now to ways to apply your sharpened abilities.

Begin by making yourself a lectern. It need be no more than a base, an upright member and a slanted top. It doesn't matter what it looks like so long as it is stable. It should be approximately forty inches high but this will vary depending on your height. The important thing is that notes placed on it be easily readable.

If you haven't the tools or the materials to build a lectern, put a box of the right height on a table. A stack of books will do.

Place the lectern in a private place in your home where you will be free to speak aloud. You will be self-conscious about speaking aloud at first and it is important that you not be distracted by concern about being overheard.

This will become the place, the very important place, where you will develop the skills needed to speak effectively in public. These skills will have a second and even more consequential function: As the ability to speak on your feet develops, you will automatically improve your ability to converse!

I cannot overstate this benefit. Effectiveness in public speaking makes for effectiveness in conversational speech — in discussions, in small meetings and in every kind of social setting.

Practicing speaking aloud

How should you begin?

Stand behind your lectern and try to imagine a group of, say, fifty people seated in front of you. The reason for this is obvious: You will not be talking to the empty air; your mind will have something to focus on.

Now, speak to your "audience" in a normal, conversational voice. Begin, by introducing yourself. Say, "Good evening. My name is John Doe. I'm thirty-six years old. I was born in Chicago. I live on the north side at 3236 Spruce Street. My parents' names are James and Margaret. My wife's name is Elizabeth but everyone calls her Liz. We have two children, John Junior and Margaret — Maggie for short. I work at Acme Advertising where I am an account manager."

What is the point of this apparently juvenile exercise? It is designed to get you past your initial self-consciousness, and to accustom you to the sound of your own voice.

Pause for a moment and and concentrate on establishing feelings of friendliness for the imaginary people seated before you. Smile at them. Don't begin again until you actually feel warmly toward them. You will be surprised at how your attitude will affect your delivery.

Repeat your speech a number of times. delivering it in different ways. Now imagine that your audience is a thousand people. You will have to raise your voice. Observe the difference in the way you addressed the larger group. Now reduce the audience to a half dozen in a conference room. See how you make the adjustment.

Practice for at least fifteen minutes a day for a week or two; longer if you feel like it.

In one session, tell your audience what you did that day. Another day, talk about the television show you watched the previous evening. Recount something interesting that happened at work. Remember to vary the size of your audiences.

"Kid stuff," you may object.

But if you have done little or no speaking in public you are as a child, and you need to learn to walk before you can run.

Variations in tone

Work for a while now on emphasis.

A majority of public speakers bore with the sound of their voice. They speak in monotones. It is flat prairie land with no hills or valleys, a kind of sustained droning. I've heard speakers who could put a hyperactive child to sleep. Conversely, notice the vitality, the liveliness in the tones of those who are accomplished in the art.

Much of the vitality of the voice has to do with the emphasis placed on words or phrases, with pauses, with variations in volume.

Here is an exercise that will teach you these rhetorical skills and help you to understand how they work. Let's work on the sentence: *Most men don't understand women.* Note how, by emphasizing each word separately, you can make the sentence take on entirely different meanings. Say it out loud.

"*Most* men don't understand women."

You are conveying through this emphasis that a few men do understand women, but that most don't.

"Most *men* don't understand women." You are now saying that, while women may understand women, a majority of men don't.

"Most men *don't* understand women." You are now contradicting someone who has said that most men do understand women.

"Most men don't *understand* women." This time you are suggesting that, while most men may appreciate women, even love them, they don't understand them.

And finally: "Most men don't understand *women*." They may understand other men, even children or dogs, but they don't understand women.

Repeat each sentence a number of times, using the different emphases, and you will see that, if you want to communicate precisely, you must not only speak coherent sentences, you must sharpen the meaning by your emphases.

Variations in volume

Let us now practice raising and lowering the voice. In this exercise, the volume and intensity of your voice will add impact to what you are saying. Read aloud this excerpt from a story:

> The man ran quickly to the prow of the boat and peered into the night.
>
> "Help!" he shouted. "Help!"
>
> He was still for a moment, listening. Again he cupped his hands to his mouth and cried out, "Help! Please! . . . Somebody help!"
>
> There was no sound but the sighing of the wind.

Now speak it this way: (Normal voice) *The man ran quickly to the prow of the boat and peered into the night.* (Moderately loud on the word, Help!) *"Help!" he shouted. "Help!"* (Normal voice) *He was still for a moment, listening.* (Slight increase in volume) *Again, he cupped his hands to his mouth and cried out,* (Loudly) *"Help! . . . Please! . . . Somebody help!"* (Quietly) *There was no sound but the sighing of the wind.*

Try it a number of times, experimenting. Try to get a sense of excitement into your voice, but avoid trying to sound like an actor. Try pausing briefly between the sentences. On the closing sentence, let your voice go flat and emotionless.

This is a difficult exercise, one that would challenge experienced speakers. Seldom will you include such dramatic moments in a speech, and seldom will you use such varying emphases. The exercise is designed to impress on you the importance of the volume and tone of your voice.

Let me emphasize as strongly as I can that the worst error you can commit as a public speaker is to ham it up.

Acting is a skill. Good acting is an art. You are not seeking to become an actor; your goal is to become an effective communicator of ideas. There are few more tiresome and obnoxious speakers than those who are in love with the sound of their voice. Naturalness is the key.

Another caution: Having begun to learn the importance of emphasizing specific words and phrases, cool it. Proper emphasis is fundamental to the communicating of precise meanings, but overemphasis is as bad as or worse than its opposite. Emphasis is most effective when it is subtle. If you are heavy-handed, if you hammer words rather than fashion them, you will draw attention to the words at the expense of their meaning.

The good golfer doesn't smash the ball, he strokes it. Good speakers don't bludgeon with words, they enlighten with ideas.

Work on it.

Preparing a speech

You are ready now to try your hand at the preparation of a speech, a brief speech three to five minutes long.

Choose any subject within your personal experience. Don't talk about "Democracy versus Communism," or "Protectionism and Free Trade." Choose instead a subject like, "This Is My City" or "My First Job." We'll discuss later how to organize a speech; for now, just have a go.

Type the speech. If you don't have access to a typewriter or a word processor, write or print it legibly because you are going to read it aloud. Don't labor over it — we'll come to that later — just get it on paper, exercising reasonable care.

Now place it on the lectern and read it aloud to your invisible audience. You will find that you want to make changes in it. Do so. Then read it aloud again.

Now examine the speech in light of your experience in reading it. You will almost certainly discover that your sentences are too long. There is nothing wrong with lengthy sentences, but they are difficult to read aloud. Trim them, either by eliminating unnecessary words or by dividing your longer sentences into two. Even three.

You may find that you have used words that are difficult to pronounce in a particular sequences. To present an extreme example, take the sentence, "Mississippians' accents sometimes leave a preponderance of Pennsylvanians perplexed." It is not particularly difficult to read but it is difficult to read aloud.

You may find that in preparing your speech you have tried to be too fancy. Instead of beginning, "It is a particular pleasure to be with you this evening," you would be better to say, "I'm glad to be here tonight."

Stay with straightforward, declarative English.

Make your revisions and then retype your speech, but with this difference: Use diagonal strokes rather than periods. You will find it much easier to read / The diagonal stroke stands out / It will catch your eye as you approach it / And it will prepare you for the end of the sentence/

Now read the revised speech aloud, trying to incorporate the various improvements we've been discussing. Continue to do so for three days. You will be pleasantly surprised at the progress you will have made. Think back to your first attempts and compare your performance now. You may still feel awkward, but is there not a marked improvement from the day you rigged your lectern and essayed your maiden effort?

Everything to this point has been prologue.

You have been struggling to rise from all fours; you are now on your feet and ready to walk. You are beginning to feel comfortable speaking aloud while standing before an audience (albeit invisible) and you have learned some of the basic rules that govern effective public speech.

Keep it up. You have no idea how skillful you will become with time.

Speaking from notes

Time now to take a giant step: namely, to stop reading aloud and to learn how to speak from notes.

Let me state it unequivocally: Reading in public is not public speaking; it is public reading. And it is, more often than not, boring.

There are rare individuals who can read a speech and hold your interest. But those who can are almost invariably people of extraordinary eminence. They hold your attention, in large part, because of who they are or because of the importance of what they are saying.

Ronald Reagan could read a speech and hold your attention, but it was because he was President of the United States, the most powerful individual in the world. He was speaking about matters that could have nationwide or worldwide repercussions. And he didn't seem to be reading.

When you saw him address the Congress or deliver a campaign speech, there were two teleprompters before him — one to either side — on which the text of his speech was projected line by line as he delivered it. And having been a professional actor, he had mastered the delivery of the written word.

He could, as the saying has it, lift the words off the page. But he is the exception. Very few "readers" can avoid boring their audience.

Speeches that are read rather than spoken suffer from two drawbacks:

(1) The speaker has his or her head down much of the time and thus has little eye contact with the listeners.
(2) The sentence structure normally used in writing is different from that used in speaking. Each has its own style.

Despite this, I am going to urge you to prepare for each speech you make by writing it first.

Writing will help you organize your thoughts and will fix your ideas in your mind. And, inasmuch as you may give a speech more than once, having it in writing will make subsequent preparations much easier.

The memorized speech

Do *not* attempt to memorize your written speech. It is a fatal error. For two reasons:

First: No matter how fondly you may believe you are masking the fact that you are speaking from memory, it will be obvious to most of your audience. Except for the most gifted actors, memorized material is made evident by the unfocused look on the face as the memorizer reads the text off the back of the eyeballs.

Second: Some distraction or your own nervousness during the delivery of your speech will inevitably intrude on your consciousness and cause your memory to falter. Panic! The next sentence won't come, and suddenly the fact that the speech is memorized becomes a source of terror. You flush, you stammer, you break out in perspiration, and your moment onstage ends in disaster.

What is your goal? Is it to impress the audience with your subject matter or your memory?

Don't take the written speech to the lectern; the temptation to read it will be too great. Its very presence would distract you.

Instead of memorizing it, reduce your written speech to notes.

The written version has been prepared primarily to organize your ideas and to fix them in your mind. The task now is to reduce them to notes which will serve as reminders of the points you wish to make and the sequence in which they come.

There are no rules for the making of notes. Find the way that suits you best. Your notes are checkpoints along a journey. Their purpose is to keep you on track. To be useful, a checkpoint should be brief, a mere memory-jogger to tell you where you are and where you need to go.

Reduce your speech to its salient points. State each point in the least possible number of words — they are to be an *aide-memoire*, not actual text. Under each major point list briefly the sub-points you will make.

You may find it helpful to type your principal points in capital letters and the sub-points in upper- and lower-case. You may wish to underline headings or use color or a Hi-Liter to draw your eye immediately to points of emphasis.

Work out your own system. The objective is to enable you to find your place immediately as you conclude one point and move to the next.

Put the notes for each major point on a three-by-five card. This reduces the amount of material before you when you glance down. As you finish with each card, simply move it to the bottom of the stack and thus keep things in order.

Don't be surreptitious about looking at your notes. Your listeners will know you have them — all the best speakers do — so make no bones about it.

Organizing your speech

Move now to the preparation of the speech.

The first task is to settle on a subject. Decide precisely what you want to put before your audience. Be specific. It is not enough to say: "I want to talk to you tonight about real estate." Personalize it: "I am going to tell you this evening how you can make money in today's real estate market." Suddenly your subject is personal, specific and intriguing.

Clarify in your mind exactly what you hope to accomplish with your speech. If the subject is murky, the speech will be also.

A speech needs a structure to be effective. Without it it will be rambling and lacking in focus. The best general rule is the one you follow in normal communication:

- Address yourself to the individual.
- Say what you have in mind.
- Summarize your main points.

In a business telephone call, for instance, what pattern do you almost automatically follow?

(1) You address yourself to the individual: "Mrs. Smith? This is Jim Brown. I want to talk to you about our new widgets."

(2) You tell her what is on your mind. "We have made a revolutionary change in our widgets . . ." You then explain the changes made and the benefits deriving from them.

(3) You conclude by summarizing what you have said and asking for her business.

The introduction

A speech develops as it grows. One thought pursued leads to other thoughts. New and interesting ideas will occur as you examine your subject. Your research will inform you and stimulate your imagination.

It is possible that you will find yourself with more to say than you have time for. When this happens, take care: In seeking to say everything, you will say nothing clearly.

Organize your material. To organize is simply to put things in order. But it is very important: it enables your listeners to follow your argument and to remember afterwards what you said. If you put your material together in a random, disjointed fashion, it will be confusing. Organize it and it will be easy to remember — easy for you and for your listeners.

Preparing a speech is very much like constructing a house. The builder selects from his materials and builds the basement first. The superstructure follows, and finally the roof. Each part develops from and rests on the previous part.

So it is with your speech. You lay the foundation, you develop it and then you cap it.

If you encounter difficulty in organizing your material, you may find it useful to list on separate pieces of paper the various points you want to make. Move them about until you find a logical progression. You will be surprised at how your points will tend to fall into place.

The preparation done, write the speech. Don't worry too much about precise wording; you aren't going to read it. You want to get your thoughts on paper, to fix them in your mind. Writing them will do more to accomplish this than any other method.

Having written the body of the speech, turn to the conclusion. The conclusion should summarize, in a most pointed manner, what you have just said. Try to distill it to three or at most a half dozen sentences. You are saying in effect: "Here in a nutshell is what I want you to carry away from the meeting."

Some years ago one of U.S. President Franklin Roosevelt's sons was scheduled to make a speech in California. He sent a telegram to the White House asking his father for counsel. Roosevelt, one of the great speechmakers in American history, sent back this advice: "Be brief, be sincere and . . . be seated."

So, your summary concluded, don't dawdle. Say "Thank you," and sit down.

First impressions

The most difficult part of a speech is the first few minutes. To grasp just how important it is, view it from the standpoint of someone in your audience. What does this person see? The chair has introduced you, a relative stranger, and you have advanced to the speaker's stand. What first impression is received? Is your appearance impressive or offputting? Do you seem quietly confident or ill at ease? Do you fuss with your notes? When you look out at your audience, do you communicate friendliness or do you seem self-conscious and nervous?

The fact is, before you speak one word you have already communicated with your audience — by your appearance and by your demeanor. If the first impression is bad, it may take you five minutes to overcome it.

It is imperative that the first impression be a good one and that your first words seize the audience's interest, so prepare yourself for it.

While you are being introduced, talk to yourself. Say, "I believe that what I am about to say is worth hearing and I believe these people will be helped by hearing it." This will add greatly to your confidence.

Next, set your mood. Summon feelings of good will. Think to yourself: These are decent people. They have expectations of me, and I must try to be informative and helpful to them. Approach the speaker's stand in this mood and it will communicate itself to your audience.

Getting off on the right foot

How should you begin?

Do not follow the common practice of saying something like: "Mr. Chairman, Madam Secretary, honored guests and ladies and gentlemen." To begin thus is to waste the opportunity to seize your audience's attention.

You may object: "But everyone begins that way; it is common courtesy."

The fact that everyone does it is a good reason for not doing it.

Despite what you may think, there is no need to do it. Nor will its omission be taken as discourtesy. I have made thousands of speeches in every circumstance imaginable and have never encountered a single instance where the chairman or any of the other dignitaries were made unhappy by my omission of the standard opening sentence.

I urge you to omit it because it is imperative that your opening sentences accomplish two things:

- They must create a good impression.
- They must command the attention of the listeners.

Too many speakers try to achieve these objectives by beginning with a joke. This is unwise. With the sense of timing and the pointed punch line that most jokes require, not everyone can tell a joke well. Most funny stories require a preamble to set up the punch line and this can quickly become tedious. Worse, many in your audience will have already heard the joke — why not; didn't *you* get it somewhere? — and your response may be groans rather than laughter.

Your opening statement must meet three criteria: It must be brief, it must capture your listeners' attention and it must have personal overtones.

EXAMPLE: Let's say your subject is real estate. You might start:

Let me begin by asking you a question. How many houses, new and used, do you think were built and sold in the Toronto area last year? 5,000? 25,000? More than 50,000?

The answer is approximately 83,000.

The total value of those houses was more than twenty-two billion dollars. The commissions earned were in excess of five and one quarter billion dollars! Perhaps those numbers will help to interest you in my subject this afternoon. It is "How You Can Make Money in Today's Real Estate Market."

Let me restate that with the proper emphasis: "How *You* Can Make Money in Today's Real Estate Market."

Can you doubt that, beginning thusly, you would have the attention of your audience?

EXAMPLE: If your subject is, say, investments, you could use a visual trick to capture your listeners' attention. You might begin by raising a hand over your head, the fist closed, and saying:

> Ladies and gentlemen, I hold here in my hand something that is the basis of all the wealth in the world.
>
> It is small, as you can see. It has little value in itself. It is useless except for the purpose for which it was created. Left to itself it will diminish in value. Used wisely, it can multiply again and again and again.
>
> (At this point you open your hand and display the object between your thumb and forefinger) It is a silver dollar.

EXAMPLE: You are slated to address a high-school assembly on the topic of AIDS. The subject is heavy and there is an air of nervous anticipation in the audience. Conscious of the tension and the delicacy of the subject matter, how should you begin? Perhaps you should try to ease the tension by approaching your subject with humor:

> Perhaps you have read the couplet,
>
> > Won't somebody give me some good advice
> > On how to be naughty and still be nice?
>
> In an odd sort of way it sums up the attitude of millions of people today to sexual morality. We say, "I know I ought to be good, and yet it's so much fun at times to be bad." St. Augustine said it perfectly some sixteen hundred years ago when he prayed, "Lord, make me pure . . . but not yet!"

Note that in all these examples, the introductory statements are pointed and not prolonged. They are informal, they are intriguing and they are personal. They have been designed to seize the listeners' interest.

Delivering your speech

We come now to the actual delivery of your speech.

Before you begin, pause until you are sure you have the attention of your audience. If you walk to the speaker's stand and immediately launch into your introduction, the audience will not be quite ready for you. An audience wants to take a first look, make a preliminary appraisal. Give them a moment to do so.

Place your notes on the lectern and stand there for a few seconds (no more than three) in a relaxed manner. Look at your audience. Think friendly thoughts as you wait. Silence will begin to settle and the anticipation will be heightened.

You are now ready to begin.

"All well and good," you may object, "but I'm going to be scared half to death. The temptation will be to drop my eyes and get started in some innocuous way."

Granted. It is not an easy moment, but it is your moment of opportunity, and by taking advantage of it you can seize upon the undivided attention of your audience and get off to a good start.

If you don't have their attention when you begin it will be a long uphill journey.

Using gestures

There can be little doubt that the appropriate gesture greatly enhances the spoken word. Watch accomplished speakers and you will observe that they supplement their speeches with body language.

Skillful orators may gently raise a forefinger to emphasize a point or form a hand into a fist and pound it into a palm. They may lean forward in earnest entreaty, spread their arms expansively, stamp a foot or stand mutely, head raised, as though appealing to the gods. The range and appropriateness of their gestures mark them as the masters they are.

But gestures are perilous territory for the amateur. Many speakers militate against their effectiveness by pointless, mechanical gestures. Most politicians, even the most eminent, suffer from this problem. They chop an arm up and down as though cutting kindling. They shake their finger or pound the podium. Most of the time, rather than supplementing what is being said, the gestures interfere with the transmission of the thought. Sometimes they become downright annoying.

I remember watching a renowned clergyman, his face beet-red, pounding his fist on the pulpit until it trembled, all the while bellowing, "God loves you!" I almost expected him to say, "God loves you, dammit!"

Gestures are risky for the neophyte and are best avoided.

Ronald Reagan seldom gestured while making a speech. If it was good enough for the so-called "Great Communicator," it will surely do for your fledgling flights.

If, regardless, you want to use gestures, don't plan them. Deliberate gestures invariably look like what they are. Leave such mannerisms to the professional actor; he has the authority of William Shakespeare to "suit the action to the word." You are not a trained actor, and if you start posturing you will betray your inexperience and distract your audience.

A caution: Even though you may have decided not to use gestures, guard against involuntary movements. Most gestures are unconscious expressions of your emotions, and in the intensity of your passion you may be unaware that you are stabbing with a forefinger or pumping your arm up and down as though trying to draw water. Ask a friend to watch for such annoying habits and to draw them to your attention.

Ask that friend, however, to wait until the following day before informing you of any excesses. You will hypersensitive to criticism, even after a good speech, and a negative note might be disheartening.

Sound systems

A good sound system is a gift from heaven; a poor one is an invention of the devil. A good system can save you from shouting yourself hoarse; a poor one can push you the edge of madness. A poor one may moan and sputter, go suddenly silent or squeal with feedback. Some microphones require you to work so close to them that your face is hidden. Others are so "live" that the rustling of notes sounds like a clashing of swords.

The function of a sound system is to make the human voice audible in every part of a room or auditorium. Most sound systems are operated at too high a level. The ideal setup simply augments

the voice so that it is clearly audible in every part of the auditorium
— *but no more*! You don't shatter eardrums in conversation; why
do it in a public speech?

Few soundmen know much about acoustics! They believe that
their job is the mere provision of amplification. They frequently
position loudspeakers at the four corners of the room on the theory
that they will thus be covering everyone in the audience. They
don't seem to understand that, in doing so, they create the impression of voices speaking from five different places.

The problem can worsen with an increase in the size of an auditorium. I recall arriving in Johnstown, Pennsylvania, to make a
major speech. I went to the arena, which seated about ten thousand,
on the afternoon of the evening meeting. My hosts were alive with
excitement; mine was to be the first speech in their spanking-new
arena. They were particularly proud of the new sound system
which had cost tens of thousands of dollars.

I went to the platform to try out the system. Disaster! The sound
engineer had installed two dozen supplementary speakers around
the perimeter of the building on the theory that, thus, everyone
would be able to hear. But the man didn't have the wit to realize
that sound travels at different speeds electronically and through the
air. My voice was arriving at the various speakers a split second
before it arrived through the air and was, as a consequence, repeating and echoing in an unintelligible jumble of sound.

The problem was solved only by turning off the entire system
and placing two powerful speakers on the platform so that my
voice and the amplified sound emanated from one place.

Even though the venue for your speech may be relatively small,
arrive ahead of time to test the system. A poor sound system can do
more to ruin a good speech than any other single thing.

Dealing with distractions

Unforeseen interruptions can interfere with your speech and so distract you and your audience that your effectiveness is destroyed.

There is the mother, usually seated in the front row, with a fret-
ful or crying child, who will not slip out of the meeting to comfort

the child, and may even slap or shake it to silence it, thus stimulating fresh paroxysms of howling.

There is the hyperactive functionary compulsively opening and closing windows and doors, stalking around holding whispered consultations, straightening rows of chairs.

There are those boorish groups of (usually) men who stand at the rear of the hall and hold extended conversations, bothering the people in the back rows.

Their name is legion.

What can you do in such circumstances?

If the problem is not too serious, try to disregard it. Focus your attention on your speech. But if the interruptions are destroying your concentration or bothering your audience, choose the appropriate moment, pause and say something like:

"I wonder, Madam, if you and the baby wouldn't be happier out in the hallway. My voice is loud, and I'm sure it's disturbing the child. Please come back when things have settled down. Thank you. Thank you very much."

You might get the officious functionary's attention by pausing and saying pleasantly: "Sir! . . . Yes, you, sir. Perhaps you would like to join the rest of audience. I think we can leave the literature table and the chairs as they are for now. Thank you for your concern."

The best thing to say to the garrulous standees at the rear of the auditorium is: "A word to you gentlemen at the rear . . . I wonder if you wouldn't prefer to finish your conversation outside in the lobby. I'm sure I must be interrupting you. Thank you, gentlemen."

Note that, in each case, you are not hostile and that you say "thank you" before they so much as move. This makes it difficult for them to refuse.

You may make people angry at you, but it has to be done. Most of the audience will be grateful and will be impressed by your ability to handle a difficult situation. Your primary objective is to be helpful to your audience. If you and they are distracted, you will end up pleasing no one.

Such drastic steps should be taken only when the meeting is being disrupted. Any public speaker must be prepared to put up with distractions, but there are limits.

At such times, there is no need to suffer fools gladly.

In concluding, I return to the answer given by the concert pianist when asked how to become skilled at the piano: "Practice your scales." I would also reiterate that good public speakers aren't born, they are made, by discipline and hard work.

Few commitments will bring greater rewards. In the process of becoming an accomplished public speaker you will improve your conversational ability, your extemporaneous skills and your qualifications to lead. And when someone must be delegated to speak for the company — to address an annual meeting, to make a presentation, to introduce a sales campaign or to lead a seminar, to appear on radio or television — you will be considered.

But such opportunities come only to those who are ready.

FOR REVIEW

(1) There are few skills more valuable than the ability to say precisely what you want to say and to say it effectively before an audience.

(2) It is surprising that there are so few good public speakers when there are so many good talkers. Public speaking is little more than a specialized form of talking.

(3) If you want to be a good concert pianist you must practice. If you want to be a good public speaker you must do the same.

(4) Train your subconscious mind to supply the appropriate words and phrases, thus freeing yourself to concentrate on the content of your speech.

(5) Learn the techniques: Practice speaking aloud, vary your tone, vary your volume, speak from notes and use gestures.

10 | Generating Word Power

L ET US LOOK AT THE TOOLS needed for effective communication.

First and foremost, words.

If you work with your mind rather than with your hands, words are the tools of your trade. (The painter, the musician and the dancer are exceptions; they communicate through the emotions.) Just as it is impossible for plumbers and carpenters to do their work without tools, so it is impossible for you to accomplish your tasks without an adequate vocabulary and some facility in its use.

A good vocabulary makes life simpler. It permits you to say exactly what you mean. Moreover:

- It equips you to communicate your ideas to others.
- It enables you to get your thoughts on paper.
- It permits you to describe not only your thoughts but your feelings.
- It qualifies you to speak on behalf of others.
- It saves time. (You don't waste time trying to correct the misunderstandings that arose because you were unable to make things plain the first time.)

A good vocabulary gives you confidence. You are more at ease in the company of others. You can join the conversation and make a contribution to it without the embarrassment of being betrayed by your inability to find the right words.

Words are power
The successful politician can go before an audience of thousands or a television audience of millions and, using the appropriate words, shape the opinions of her listeners.

The novelist is able to sit isolated at his typewriter and, using his mastery of words, move the minds and the emotions of men and women he will never meet.

A Winston Churchill can rise in the British House of Commons and, using nothing but words, change an irresolute Britain into a heroic and united nation.

Words are the servants of the mind
They are messengers that carry your thoughts to others, and disclose your interests and intentions. By using words, you can transmit your inmost feelings; lacking them, you may stand dumb in time of crisis. They can be loyal servants or they can betray you.

Words are the tools of thought
It is impossible to think clearly without them. The larger your vocabulary the more capable you are of creative thought. The illiterate may be able to intuit an idea but be unable to articulate it clearly, and so it dies with him. This is true no matter how profoundly or intensely the idea may be felt. This does not mean that an individual with a large vocabulary is necessarily a creative thinker; it does mean that that individual has the potential to be.

Words are inspiring
A young man in his early thirties, the son of a carpenter, without formal education, can begin to speak about God and life in the towns and byways of his country and so move his hearers that his ideas may still be said to be the most influential in the history of the Western world.

Words are the heart of human relationships
Words make it possible to communicate the simplest and the most profound emotions. Words can bless or curse. Words can free or enslave. They can articulate the anger of a dockworker or the repentance of a King David. They can spew hate or murmur love. They can voice a nursery rhyme or proclaim a Shakespeare sonnet. They can inculcate loyalty or incite rebellion. The civilized society rests on words.

Words are money
A group of researchers at the Human Engineering Laboratory in the United States conducted a series of tests on a variety of individuals, seeking to understand the importance of a knowledge of words. The men and women tested were drawn from most of the professions. The objective was to determine the extent of each subject's vocabulary.

The test was prepared by Alexander Ingles of the Graduate School of Education at Harvard University and was relatively simple. The subject was provided with one hundred and fifty selected words, each presented in a brief phrase and italicized to distinguish it. The subject was then given five possible synonyms for the italicized word and asked to indicate which was closest in meaning. These were the results:

- Three hundred high school freshmen averaged seventy-five errors.
- Seven hundred and fifty college freshmen averaged forty-two errors.
- One thousand college graduates averaged twenty-seven errors.
- A group of professional academics averaged eight errors.
- A group of senior businessmen — all of them top-drawer executives who had been for five years or more the chairperson or chief executive officer of their companies — averaged seven errors.

The Human Engineering Laboratory reached many conclusions — among them that a large vocabulary is a common characteristic in almost all successful individuals, regardless of occupation.

Not all the businessmen tested had pursued formal education to its limits; one of them had ended his schooling at the age of fourteen. Incidentally, he scored only two errors in the one hundred and fifty questions.

One conclusion that can be drawn from the test results is that the executives who did well had realized early in life the power of words. They had acquired the ability to use words to communicate their ideas and their wishes. When they addressed the public, their associates, their clients and their subordinates, they were able to explain precisely what they wanted and to digest the information they were given.

(Incidentally, the tests appeared to demonstrate that the breadth of the English vocabulary of business executives had a direct relationship to the money they earned. The larger the vocabulary, the larger the paycheck.)

A limited vocabulary handicaps

Words!

Welcome them, get acquainted with them, give them good company, and they will open life to you and open you to others.

Without a knowledge of them, you are in a very real sense handicapped. Your brain is diminished. Your hearing is impaired and your tongue is tied. You are like a person with a hearing loss who misses half of what is being said, like someone with a speech impediment unable to articulate his or her thoughts.

To grasp the fearsome handicap you suffer when you lack the words you need to say what you intend, visualize yourself lost in China, all your identification stolen. Your dilemma is profound. You try to explain your problem, but no one understands what you are saying. Nor can anyone assist you, for you don't understand them. You are anxious, confused and frustrated, but you have no way to communicate your feelings. Whether you speak them or write them, your words have no meaning. You are, in effect, deaf and dumb. Unable to speak, you find yourself thrust back a million years in time, reduced to primitive grunts and gestures.

Do I overstate the case? Perhaps. But in hinterlands China or at home, if you haven't the words to say what you want to say you are impaired in your relations with others. However much you may want to, you can't get your ideas, your feelings, your intentions across and other people can't effectively communicate with you.

But the problem is even more profound than that: A limited vocabulary limits your ability to think.

It is not merely that you are incapable of communicating clearly; your thoughts are hazy. What you have in your mind is murky, inexplicit, confused. When you try to grasp a complex idea, you become bewildered.

The teenager studding his sentences with "You know . . ." doesn't himself quite know. He has vague notions about what he wants to communicate and resorts to "You know . . ." in the hope that you will surmise what he is thinking but isn't able to articulate.

Determine to shake off the handicap. Every word you add to your vocabulary will heighten the meaning of your life.

Building a vocabulary

How does one go about increasing one's store of words?

First and most important, you must want to.

Not only at this moment, when the importance and the power of words are being emphasized and when high resolves are stirring, but as a deep conviction. You must become convinced of the importance of an increased vocabulary to you.

If it is your earnest wish, and not a mere whim, to be successful in business and in human relationships, your desire must be transformed into determination. Wishes won't make it so.

Nor will your goals be easily achieved. They will be more difficult for some than for others. The important thing to remember is this: They aren't impossible for anyone.

So perhaps before we proceed you should put this book down and go off by yourself somewhere. Take stock of yourself. Measure the strength of your determination.

You may find yourself offering excuses: "My English is lousy. My dad didn't have much schooling, neither did my mom, and I didn't finish high school. I'm starting behind the eight ball."

It is undeniably a fact that the quality of the language spoken in the home is probably the most important contributor to a skill with words. If your parents were limited in their knowledge of words, your challenge will be greater than that faced by some others.

My upbringing turned me toward words. On weekends, the house was filled with Irishmen, recent immigrants to Canada, associates of my father's, in the Robert Simpson Company in Regina, Saskatchewan. The Irish love to talk; they exult in disputation. My father's friends would come on their days off work, mostly on Saturdays or Sundays, to join my father for a drink and a bout of conversation.

I would find a chair close by the circle of men — the women had gone to the kitchen. I was allowed to stay as long as I didn't fidget or swing my feet or speak.

Their games were played with words. They threw out opinions, challenged each other's assertions and wrestled, often hotly, with meanings.

On one of these occasions, my father announced that he was prepared to prove "through unassailable logic" that black was white. Which, using a sequence of carefully planned syllogisms, he proceeded to do. The achievement set off a boisterous debate, but I was oblivious to it. I was puffed with pride at my father's achievement and entranced with the wonder of it all.

That was the positive side of my childhood. The negative was that I dropped out of school at seventeen and had to develop my love of words by myself.

If you are tempted to despair by your lack of an adequate vocabulary, consider how great your advantages are. Compare your problem with the problems faced by European and Asiatic immigrants when they come to our world, most of them speaking no English when they arrive but thousands of them going on to outstanding achievement.

Never too late to start

It may be that your school days, with their regimen of study, are long gone and that you aren't sure you can find in yourself the discipline required.

Perhaps you can't, but how will you know if you don't try?

And don't argue that learning is more difficult in the middle years. A case can be made for the opposite view. For example, there are fewer distractions for the middle-aged than for men and women in their twenties.

The late teens and early adult years, with all their uncertainties, with their hectic social agenda and with their leaner income, are behind you. Your days may be as full now as they were then but you have acquired some wisdom and some judgment in the intervening years. You are more aware that "life is real, life is earnest." And you are impressed with the importance of being equipped for success. Beyond that, there are countless examples of men and women who discovered that the middle and the later years are the best years in which to grow.

The problem is not as great as it seems. When we face any major obstacle, we tend to see it as a whole. And this can be intimidating. But few problems are overcome holus-bolus; they are dealt with one step at a time.

If you contemplate the work necessary to become proficient in English, you will be intimidated. But if you determine only to begin, you will be surprised at how swift — and pleasurable — your progress will be.

There will be a thousand reasons for postponing the new beginning but none of them will be valid unless you believe them.

And if you really do believe success is beyond you, or that it is easily achieved, why did you buy this book?

If you don't move now to improve yourself, when will you?

The basic tools

We begin our quest to improve our ability with words with a simple and universally available aid, a dictionary.

If you don't own a dictionary, buy one. Not a massive volume intended to rest on a lectern, but a slim version; one that will fit into your pocket or your purse.

Rule one: Read one page of your dictionary every day.

Without fail.

It can be done at any time of the day but I recommend last thing at night. When you come upon a word you don't understand, speak it aloud. (If you need to, check the phonetic guide; you'll find it at the beginning of the dictionary, or at the bottom of each page.) Voice each word not once but a half dozen times.

You are seeking to create a working vocabulary, and speaking the word will help lodge it in your mind and make you more comfortable with it.

After you sound the word, read its definition or definitions (some words have more than one). Fix three facts in your mind: the word, its pronunciation, its meaning.

Depending on the size of your vocabulary, you may find anywhere from two to a dozen unfamiliar words on a page. Don't try to learn more than three words a day. Better to lodge three new words securely in your brain than to expose yourself to a larger number and not know their meaning. And don't disdain the adding of three words a day. At that rate you will learn twenty-one new words a week, more than a thousand words a year.

No small achievement.

Some people will be able to learn more than three words a day; others will have to settle for fewer. Set your own pace, but be certain you make the unfamiliar words yours before moving on.

You should add another book to your armory: a thesaurus. Sounds like a prehistoric lizard, but a thesaurus is merely a book that lists words similar in meaning to the word you look up.

For example, if you look up the word "similar" you find a list including "akin," "like," "alike," "comparable," "matching," "related," and "same." The function of a thesaurus is to help you find the exact word you need. It is an invaluable tool, and you should become familiar with it.

No professional writer who wants to communicate exact meanings would attempt to do so without a dictionary and a thesaurus at hand. And, although writing may not be your primary business, you should familiarize yourself with both books and refer to one or the other every time you come upon a word you don't understand.

Can the average adult reasonably hope to build a large and serviceable vocabulary? There is evidence that it can be done. Compare, for instance, a typical first-year student in law school and a graduate.

The neophyte sounds very much like any other undergraduate. Her grammar is adequate, but not much more. Her pronunciations are sloppy. Her syntax is casual. But talk to her at graduation and you will observe that a radical change has taken place. Her words are articulated clearly — often to the point of seeming labored. Her sentences cohere; her syntax is much improved.

What has happened? The wet-behind-the-ears freshman has had it drummed into her head that, in the practice of law, she must speak with precision. She has consequently worked hard to achieve that goal. You will see similar changes in most aspirants to a profession — academics, doctors, business majors. They have learned that, when they deal with students or patients or associates, it is imperative to communicate exact meanings.

You may not plan to be a doctor or a lawyer, but you may aspire to be a merchant chief. If you are going to be successful in your field, you will need to acquire some of the same skills in language that your counterparts achieve in the professions.

The painless way to word power

A painless way to increase your vocabulary is through reading. Not only is it painless, it can be one of life's great pleasures.

Reading is the easiest and the most natural way to expand your vocabulary and your ability to speak and write. It is not a coincidence that the brightest and most articulate people are almost invariably avid readers. Nothing compares with reading as a way to increase your conversational and writing skills.

The suggestion that you begin reading regularly may be off-putting. You may think "Reading is hard work. In high school or college, when reading was mandatory, it was often boring and tiresome."

But don't read as a duty; read whatever you fancy. Have a go at Mark Twain or Charles Dickens. Sample Anthony Burgess or Ernest Hemingway or Norman Mailer or Robertson Davies. You may find that you enjoy Robert Frost's poems. Try a P.D. James detective story or a Stephen King thriller. Pick up one of the classics. Browse in the paperback section in a bookstore or a supermarket. Buy what appeals to you.

Can't afford to buy books? Borrow them from the public library.

What should you read? Anything and everything. Everything from Shakespeare to the Reader's Digest to the newsmagazine to the back of a cereal box. There is no more useful leisure activity. Cut back on your television viewing and read.

Make your reading purposeful. As you are reading, you will find unfamiliar words. The context of the new words will usually make their meanings evident and it may seem unnecessary to look them up. Nonetheless, do so. If you look them up, you will make them familiar friends, rather than strangers encountered and forgotten.

Many people don't interrupt their reading to look up words: they keep paper and pencil nearby. Jot down the unfamiliar word and the page number, and look up the word later. Get over the lazy habit of breezing past words you don't understand.

Reading can be like an enjoyable walk through a field in springtime, gathering flowers as you go.

As your vocabulary grows — and you will be surprised at how quickly it does — use it. Try out new words around family and friends. Then as your confidence grows, use them elsewhere.

Don't draw back because you are afraid to make mistakes. (Remember how awkward you were when you were learning to ride a bicycle — and how effortless it became?) You will be surprised at how swiftly you progress.

You may be tempted to try to impress others by introducing uncommon words into your conversation. Don't. You might blunder, and you'll almost certainly seem pretentious or foolish.

The so-called "big words" have little to do with everyday conversation. Yes, people who are skilled with language do use polysyllabic words, but only if those words are essential. The best communication is direct and straightforward speech that does not try to impress. The deliberate use of an exotic word will only draw attention to the word and to you. It will get in the way of what you are trying to say.

The most effective speakers are those who impress on their audience the content of their message, not the extent of their vocabulary. Big words are not necessary if you want to sway your listeners.

Abraham Lincoln's Gettysburg Address is widely regarded as one of the great speeches of modern times, yet it is notable for its economy of language. Here is its conclusion:

> . . . that we here highly resolve that these dead shall not have died in vain; that this nation, under God, shall have a new birth of freedom, and that government of the people, by the people, for the people, shall not perish from the earth.

Jesus of Nazareth was a master storyteller. But note the simplicity of language as he begins his parable of the prodigal son:

> There was a man who had two sons. The younger of them said to his father, 'Father, give me the share of property that falls to me.' And he divided his capital between them. Not many days later, the younger son took all he had and took his journey into a far country, and there he wasted his money in loose living.

Only three words with more than two syllables (and they with only three), but how perfectly the story is begun!

In some ways I was lucky to be born before the invention of radio and television. We had the usual childish games, but otherwise our amusements were limited to a few scratchy seventy-eight-rpm records and to books — plus the Saturday comics, of course. Fortunately, there were lots of books. I well remember one bookcase that contained Elliot's Five Foot Shelf of Fiction — yes, someone sold fiction by the foot! I began at inch one and read through the entire five feet — Dickens and the Brontës and Lawrence and Kipling and Stevenson and Wells.

Because of the Great Depression, I dropped out of school after grade nine. But the love of words that was kindled in childhood deepened and intensified. Later, I hosted a weekly CBS television show; I spoke to tens of thousands from public platforms in Canada, the United States and Western Europe; I became the managing editor of a metropolitan newspaper; and I published ten books.

All of it based on a love affair with words.

Why should *you* trouble to build a vocabulary?

Because it can help you to succeed in business, and that is the subject under discussion here. Beyond that, a love of words can add new dimensions to your life. A treasury of words enables you to think more clearly and more expansively, and to express your thoughts precisely.

You will become more fully alive.

FOR REVIEW

(1) Words are power. Words are the servants of the mind. Words are the tools of thought. Words can inspire. Words are the heart of human relationships. Civilized societies rest on words.

(2) If you work with your mind rather than with your hands, words are the tools of your trade. It is impossible to accomplish most important tasks without an adequate vocabulary and some facility in its use.

(3) A limited vocabulary limits your ability to think. Your thoughts are hazy. What you may have in mind is felt, but it is murky and inexplicit.

(4) The best tools for building a vocabulary are reading and using a dictionary and a thesaurus.

(5) The Human Engineering Laboratory, after a series of experiments, concluded that a large vocabulary is a common characteristic in almost all successful individuals, and that there was a direct relationship between the breadth of the vocabulary of business executives and the money they earned.

11 | Communicating on Paper

NEXT IN IMPORTANCE to your ability to communicate effectively through speech is your ability to communicate effectively on paper.

When you speak well you make a good impression on the people in your presence. When you write well you create a good impression in your absence.

The spoken word dies in the air or is altered by memory; the written word perseveres unchanged.

To impress others with what you *say*, you have to be there. Express your thoughts on paper — whether in a letter, a report, a memorandum, a résumé, a presentation or whatever — and you *don't* have to be there. Your written communication can be working for you in dozens of places without your having left the office.

The written word enables you to impress someone at a distance, even someone you have never met — as, for instance, in a letter or a job application or a request for an interview. You can reach people you might never be able to meet. A cat can look at a king and you can address a president.

The written word enables you to communicate with those who work for you, to forward a suggestion to a senior official, to send an introductory note before calling on a client.

A carefully drafted letter or résumé will open doors that cannot be opened in any other way. A concise, well-written memorandum can awaken superiors to your capabilities. If you have a proposal to put before the boss, put it in writing. It is not uncommon for someone in the presence of the person in charge to get the jitters and as a consequence to fail to communicate clearly. It is sometimes useful to put on paper the proposal you plan to put forward verbally and to leave it behind as an explicit reminder.

As you move up the ladder and become responsible for the actions taken by others, you will discover that, in directing them, no system is as efficient as written instruction. Verbal directives may be inexact. Or they may be exact and be misunderstood.

So put it in writing.

Fixing ideas in the mind

Beyond that, learning to write well will improve your thinking.

The act of writing forces you to think through and to organize your thoughts. Having committed your ideas to paper you will yourself understand them better and be better able to verbalize them. When you have to present important ideas to others, it is good practice to first put them down on paper.

You'll get it right if you write it first.

The act of putting your thoughts on paper will fix them in your mind and help you to be more organized and succinct when you speak.

"Ah," you say, "but I can't write. I don't seem able to get started. And my grammar is awful."

William Randolph Hearst, the renowned publisher, disagreed. Faced with such a disclaimer, he said bluntly,

"Anyone who can think can write." And, of course, he is right. If you have ideas worth expressing and you can communicate them in conversation, there is no reason why you can't learn to express them in writing. It is primarily a matter of acquiring the skill.

Observe the stumbles and falls of a baby learning to walk. After a few inept attempts, the baby would be justified in looking up at her parents and saying, "I'll *never* learn to walk." But she will. And beyond that, she will learn to run!

Oftentimes, when we are speaking, we can't come up with the right word and thus may cause misunderstandings. Or we may be imprecise in our choice of words and create confusion. In writing, you can say exactly what you intend.

For these and other reasons it is wise to follow any important meeting with a written summary of what conclusions were reached or what agreements were arrived at.

To do so is to avoid misunderstanding. Because the spoken word is so often "misspoken" or misunderstood or only partially understood, summarizing a consensus on paper permits all parties to confirm precisely what happened.

Then, if anyone has misinterpreted the agreement, the summarizing memorandum will raise questions while the discussion is fresh and matters can easily be straightened out.

Normally, after agreement has been reached, the parties involved take specific actions. These actions may have far-reaching ramifications, and if time passes before a misunderstanding is corrected, the problem can grow and even become insoluble.

It is good practice also to follow important telephone conversations with a note confirming any consensus reached. Memory is short. Our words die in the air. Moreover, because extemporized speech may be inexact, we often fail to say precisely what we mean. And even if we do state our position exactly, the person listening may hear something other than what was intended.

The laws of writing

Most of us are better talkers than we are writers. In conversation, we may be able to convince others of our views, but when we are required to put our thoughts on paper, we find ourselves struggling with the form, the words, the grammar and the punctuation.

If you have trouble expressing yourself in writing, take steps immediately to change the situation. If you are going to be successful in your business relationships you will have to learn to write well.

There are two fundamental laws about writing:

(1) You learn to write by writing.
(2) You learn to write well by rewriting.

Many draw back from the challenge of writing because they don't understand that writing is a process. We quail before the writing task because we assume that the requirement is to get it right the first time.

Absolutely wrong! You learn to write well by rewriting. You get past what has been called "the intimidation of the blank page" by beginning. So stop waiting for that thought to be perfectly formed in your mind: get your first sentence down on paper and then go to work.

I repeat: The most important thing to be said about the writing process is this: *There is no such thing as good writing; there is only good rewriting!*

No one in history ever wrote anything worth reading that was not revised, usually many times. It was true of Shakespeare, Milton, Hugo, Chekhov, Flaubert, Joyce, Shaw, Faulkner and Hemingway. They wrote and rewrote until they were satisfied that they had stated exactly what they intended.

In the words of Alexander Pope:

True ease in writing comes from art, not chance,
As he moves easiest who has learned to dance.

Mario Puzo, author of *The Godfather*, put it succinctly:

"It's all in the rewrite."

So get your thoughts on paper no matter how awkward they may seem. The person to whom you are writing will never see your first draft, so don't flinch if it is stilted or imprecise or lacks grace.

Your first draft is the raw material from which the final document will be formed.

In the spring of 1980 I wrote a novel, *Beatitudes*, in which Joshua Crown, a Mohawk Indian high-steeler, was the protagonist. He was a Christ-figure, an earthbound man whose aspirations ended in tragedy. The typescript ran to some five hundred pages, but the book wouldn't jell and I set it aside.

I took up the project again in 1985, changed the plot, did a massive rewrite and introduced a new protagonist. The title of the book was *Mr. Nobody*. My publisher rejected it. Finally, in 1988 — the protagonist now a television evangelist and Joshua Crown a subsidiary character — it was published under the title, *World of One*. The revisions and rewrites had brought the number of typewritten pages to more than four thousand.

Begin by beginning

Enough of generalizing.

Imagine that you are at your typewriter or word-processor or have your pen in hand and want to commit your thoughts to paper. How to begin?

There is a temptation to sit there chewing your pencil or gazing at the computer screen waiting for inspiration or waiting until the first sentence forms in your mind. This is a common mistake. You are not about to carve your words in stone; get them on paper.

I will let you in on a secret: The best writers are the slowest writers. It is not uncommon for a professional writer to revise each sentence and paragraph a dozen or more times. The greatest books went through a number of drafts before they were published. The words on the page seem inevitable, but they're not; they are the result of hard work.

You aren't unique when you have trouble writing well; everyone does. So don't be deterred when the right words won't come. No one but you is going to see your first draft, so begin.

In business writing, the best style is the most direct and intelligible. Your objective is to get information from your mind to someone else's mind as accurately as possible.

Disregard how inept your first attempt may seem; get started and keep going. Get your main points on paper. Continue until you have run out of things to say.

Now, beginning with the first sentence, review what you have written, revising as you go. Replace words or clauses. Restate a murky thought. If a word seems awkward, try others in its place.

Read again what you have written. Ask yourself: Do I introduce clearly what I want to say and then develop it? Does each paragraph move the subject forward? Would the sequence be improved if, say, I shifted paragraph five to paragraph three?

When you have a satisfactory version, go over it one final time and take out every word and sentence that can be cut without altering the meaning. I have rarely seen a piece of writing — other than that done by professionals — that would not be improved by cutting. It may seem like dismembering your baby, but it will improve the end product.

Guard against the most common sin of writers: falling in love with your own words.

The athlete who wants to win a race strips to the bare essentials. He may be tempted to wear his medals or to dress in fancy attire to impress the spectators, but he doesn't do so. He knows they will be most impressed by one thing: his winning the race. To achieve this, he gets rid of anything unnecessary.

When you write you will be tempted to show off your vocabulary or to try to impress with fancy phrases. Don't yield to it. Anything that interferes with or intrudes on what you want to say is excess baggage.

I am not suggesting that you write like a third-grader. Any idea can be communicated in many ways, some more graceful than others. So don't take the counsel offered here to an extreme and descend to pidgin-English. Say what you have to say in a way that suits the occasion and reflects your personality. But don't lose sight of your objective: *to convey from your mind to someone else's mind what you have in mind.*

Everything else is embellishment.

Read your report again, this time examining your paragraphs. A paragraph may be defined as "a segment of a written composition that consists of one or more sentences, deals with one point or gives the words of one speaker." Generally, you change paragraphs when you change topics. Note that the paragraph preceding this one consists of only four words, while the one you are reading contains four sentences.

As you can see, there are no inviolable rules.

To present an extreme example: In James Joyce's *Ulysses*, the final paragraph in the book runs to more than fifty pages! The preceding paragraph comprises one word, "Where?"

But you are not writing literature, you are writing for business purposes. So keep your sentences and paragraphs short. (This is not a rule; it is an aid to clear communication.) The principal reason for trying to write succinctly is to assist your readers, to keep them from losing their way while they try to follow your thought.

The problem of punctuation

"Well and good," you may say, "but the writing process isn't my problem. I am able to say what I want to, but I am at sea when it comes to punctuating what I write."

Relax. Punctuation is a subsidiary skill and few master its intricacies. There are few absolute laws. You need only to understand the *function* of punctuation: to bring order out of chaos, to so break up the words, phrases and sentences in written material that the meaning is clear.

Observe how punctuation can clarify meaning. Here are the words of several sentences strung together without punctuation: That that is is that that is not is not is not that it it is.

Punctuate it and the meaning is revealed: "That that is, is. That that is not, is not. Is not that it? It is."

It is a trick example, of course, but it emphasizes how punctuation brings sense to a sentence. Enough to say that you can learn to use punctuation in part simply by observing the punctuation in what you read. Incidentally, the simplest way to check your punctuation is to read aloud what you have written.

In your reading, pause briefly at each comma or dash. Take a breath at each semicolon, colon or period. Listen as you read. Is the meaning conveyed? Is the thought clearly expressed? Does your writing communicate exactly what you intended? If it sounds disjointed, remove some of the punctuation and read it again. You'll soon get the feel of it.

Your objective is not to demonstrate your mastery of punctuation; it is to communicate what you have in mind.

If it sounds good, leave it.

Getting temporary help

Writing skills cannot be acquired overnight, so seek interim help.

Enlist an ally. It may be a spouse, a secretary, a friend, even a daughter or son, but find someone who can help put your sentences into acceptable shape.

Have a candid talk with that person. Explain your resolve to improve your writing and enlist his or her aid for the immediate future. Don't be hesitant to state the problem — it's nothing to feel self-conscious about. Then formalize some arrangement to have your written efforts reviewed regularly.

Incidentally, don't concern yourself that you will be confessing a secret deficiency. If your helper has worked with you in any reasonably close relationship, he or she will be aware of it.

But don't make the mistake of dumping the problem on somebody else and doing nothing about it yourself. All arrangements end or alter, and if you continue to depend on someone else you may one day, perhaps at a time of crisis, find yourself without your "good right hand."

Nor can you turn the task of writing over to a subordinate. It is not enough to say, for instance: "Look, draft a letter for me saying thus and so and suggesting that we need to do this or that."

Your amanuensis may do the writing for you but he or she can't do your thinking for you. So, no matter how forbidding the task, write the first draft yourself. Remember, the act of writing will help you organize and refine your thoughts. No other exercise is so useful for this purpose.

Stay with it; you will be pleasantly surprised at your progress.

FOR REVIEW

(1) There are two fundamental laws in writing: You learn to write by writing. You learn to write well by rewriting.

(2) When you speak well you make a good impression on those in your presence. When you write well you create a good impression in your absence.

(3) No form of communication is as efficient as written instruction. Verbal directives may be inexact, or they may be exact and be misunderstood.

(4) The very act of writing forces you to think through and organize your thoughts. Having committed your ideas to paper you will understand them better.

(5) Get your thoughts on paper no matter how awkward they may seem. The person to whom you are writing will never see the first draft.

(6) Good writing and good speech are twins; they are the children of reading.

(7) The best style, in business writing, is the most direct and intelligible. The principal reason for writing clearly and succinctly is to assist the reader.

(8) The simplest way to check your punctuation is to read aloud what you have written.

12 | The Courage to Dare

THE WORLD IS FULL of people who play it safe.

This chapter is about daring, taking a chance, believing in yourself enough to go out on a limb.

I am not speaking of recklessness, of derring-do, nor of casting caution to the winds in your determination to get ahead.

That isn't daring, it's foolhardiness.

What we will consider here is the need at certain times in life to take dramatic and courageous action; but taking it only after careful consideration of the risks and the likelihood of success.

The big winners in life are the people who, when the opportunity arises, are willing to take a chance. Interestingly enough, most of the ones I have met are disciplined, thoughtful people.

Daring, not recklessness

I have a friend, a man of fertile mind and great talent. A graph of the ups and downs in his life would look like a profile of the Alps. He takes risks frequently, although, oddly, he is not what is commonly thought of as a gambler. He would, for instance, never bet on the horses or go on a junket to Las Vegas.

I have known him to fall into conversation with a stranger in the adjoining seat of an airplane and invest half a million dollars on a project that went up like a rocket and came down like a charred stick. I have known him when he rode about in a chauffeured Rolls Royce and when, one day, he borrowed my car because he didn't have the price of a bus ticket from Chicago to Detroit. Happily, he had one more up than down; when I last heard from him he was living in a luxurious penthouse apartment in Maui.

I don't think of him as daring, however; I think of him as reckless.

Contrast him with another man of my acquaintance, an experienced and imaginative young television producer on the CTV television network, whom I shall call Perry. He had worked for me the previous year and was prepared to sign for a second year except that he had been informed that Fidel Castro — then mounting his revolution in the Sierra Maestra mountains of Cuba — was willing to give him an exclusive interview. NBC television had told Perry that it would fund the venture and pay him handsomely for an exclusive.

But there was a problem. Confirmation of the Castro interview was slow in coming. Awaiting it, Perry was, understandably, unwilling to commit to me. I, too, had a dilemma: I had to have three film crews in the field by early August or I would not be ready to open the new television season. I was sympathetic to Perry — the Castro interview undoubtedly would launch him on a brilliant career with NBC — but I had deadlines to meet.

After many delays, I gave Perry an ultimatum of sorts: He would have to commit by the following weekend or I would have to hire someone else. As I spelled it out, he literally squirmed in his chair with indecision.

On the weekend, he came to see me. He apologized for the delays and for his indecision, then said he had decided to sign a contract with me.

I looked across the desk at him and said, "Sorry, the job is no longer open."

"What do you mean?" he said. "Isn't today the deadline?"

"Yes," I said, "but I've hired someone else."

His jaw dropped. "But I don't understand."

"Perry," I said,"you are taking the job with me only because you don't want to turn it down and then perhaps find that the Castro interview is no go. I can't let you do that. If you come to work for me and the Cuban shoot comes through, you will always look back on it as having blown your big chance. I'm going to presume to make the decision for you. You're twenty-seven. You're good. You have a bright future. If the Castro interview doesn't happen, other good things will. Take a chance. Dare."

Castro never did agree to the interview, but Perry later formed his own film company. He has been successful beyond his expectations.

Unrealized possibilities

Perry is an example of those who, facing an opportunity, pull back because it involves risk. He had the ability to succeed, but had he not been driven to it, he might never have found in himself sufficient resolution to form his own company and thus start down the road to success.

Too many of us are like that.

The world is full of people with potential who never realize it. Preeminent among the reasons is undue caution.

They know they are capable of doing better, but they never get out in front. They have as much ability as many of the people above them on the ladder of success, but they soldier on below. They see opportunities but don't grasp them. They watch an old friend hit it big and wonder why they can't. They come up with the occasional "million-dollar idea" but never get it off the ground.

These people have brains. They have ability. But they're going nowhere.

Their problem is, in large part, inertia.

And fear.

Inertia is the tendency of an object to continue in the state it is in unless acted upon by an outside force. The law of inertia obtains with people, too — with you, perhaps. To make a significant change in your job will probably take firm resolution and a mighty effort.

Faced with the dilemma of whether to take a certain action, an action that may involve some risk, we sometimes find ourselves immobilized by indecision. In such circumstances, conventional wisdom will usually counsel, "Don't act rashly. There is a very real possibility of failure here. Don't take a chance."

Often that will be wise counsel. But as author-clergyman William Ellery Channing has said, "There are times when . . . to dare is the highest wisdom."

Usually, we hesitate to take the leap of faith because we lack faith in ourselves. Often, that doubt arises out of the fact that we are acutely aware of our own inadequacies. We know all too well that we are cautious by nature, that we tend to postpone difficult decisions and that we are sometimes indolent. Those occasions when, in a crisis, we were indecisive and irresolute stay fresh in the memory.

But what makes you think others are more resolute than you are? If you knew them as well as you know yourself you might be appalled by their bad habits and frailties. It is entirely possible that their tentativeness exceeds yours.

The trouble is that yours are specific and all too familiar; theirs are unknown to you and insubstantial.

The probability is that you and "that other person" are cut from the same cloth, and that in a showdown you could go against him *mano a mano* with an equal chance of success.

What you need is a dash of daring.

Making the impossible happen

At the depths of the Great Depression, his family on welfare, a young Toronto artist desperately needed money. He specialized in charcoal portraits. He was good, but the times were bad. How could he make his talents pay off? Where, in hard times, were there people ready to buy an unknown's drawings?

He could canvass his neighbors and friends, but they were as strapped for cash as he was. The only possible market was among people who had money. But who? And how could he get to them?

He thought about it long and hard and finally went to the Toronto *Globe and Mail,* where he borrowed from "the morgue," the newspaper's photograph file, the official portrait of the president of the largest bank in Canada. He went home and sat down to work.

The drawing finished, he mounted it. It was good, he was confident of that. But how could he get it to his subject?

He had no friends in business, so a referral was impossible. He knew that if he tried to make an appointment he would be turned down. A letter requesting an interview would probably not get past the great man's secretary. Being something of a student of human nature, the young artist knew that his only hope of penetrating the barriers around the busy executive would be through an appeal to the man's vanity.

He decided to take an unorthodox approach. Better to try and fail than to abandon the task without trying. So he would dare.

Hair freshly trimmed, dressed in his best, he went to the president's office and asked to see him. The secretary told him it would not be possible to see the president without an appointment.

"Too bad," the young artist said, folding back the protective cover of the picture, "I wanted to show him this." The secretary looked at it, took the picture in hand and after a moment of indecision said, "Have a seat. I'll be with you in a moment."

She returned shortly. "He'll see you," she said.

The president was admiring the sketch as the artist entered. "You do excellent work," he said. "What would you charge for this?" The young man drew a deep breath, told him twenty-five dollars and the sale was made. (Twenty-five dollars then would be the equivalent of at least five hundred today.)

Why had the young artist's plan worked?

- He had worked hard to become good at what he did.
- He was imaginative: He didn't try to make an appointment by telephone, knowing he would be turned down.
- He was intrepid: Rather than try to sell to his next-door neighbor, he went to the top.
- He was insightful: He knew he had to appeal to the great man's

vanity and was wise enough to copy the official portrait, knowing the subject had approved it.

• He was enterprising. After he made the sale, he asked the bank president to recommend him to a friend.

He succeeded by daring to do the unorthodox thing, by studying his market before he acted and by thinking beyond the first sale.

And he wasn't afraid to dare to do "what simply isn't done."

Preparation precedes achievement

When you dare something and succeed at it, it is seldom the result of luck. It is more likely the consequence of imaginative thought and careful planning.

One of the greatest feats of daring I know of was Charles Lindbergh's solo flight across the Atlantic Ocean in 1927. Lindbergh, just twenty-five years old, coolly bet his life that he could triumph over what appeared to be prohibitively high odds.

Having had no sleep the night before, he took off from Long Island, New York, in a single-engine aircraft, a plane so crammed with extra tanks of gasoline that there was barely room for him in the cockpit and so borne down by the weight of the fuel that it barely got airborne, to fly from New York to Paris.

Fog obscured his vision much of the way. He had no radio to give him bearings, only a compass. A number of times he fell asleep, once to awaken only a few feet above the waves. But thirty-three hours after taking off, flying by dead reckoning, he swept in to a perfect landing at Le Bourget airport. The outburst of worldwide adulation has seldom been equalled.

Daring? Incredibly so.

Reckless? Absolutely not.

Over a period of years Lindbergh had done everything possible to prepare himself and his plane, the *Spirit of St. Louis*, for the flight. He had dropped out of the University of Wisconsin to study flying. He had trained as a flying cadet. He had earned a commission in the Air Force reserve to get free flying time. He had logged tens of thousands of miles as a United States airmail pilot in daylight and darkness, in fair weather and foul. In emergencies, he had set down in farmers' fields. He had learned how to service the engine of his plane and knew every working part.

"Lucky Lindy," the news media called him. "He gambled and he won," they said. No! He succeeded not because the dice came up right but because, before he ventured, he had prepared himself and his plane to the limit of his ability.

He was confident that he would succeed. He knew the only thing that could defeat him was a quirk of fate — and that is something none of us can control.

So, having prepared, he dared.

This is something you can do, too.

The fear of the unorthodox

There are millions of competent men and women who work hard and give their best but who go through their business life unnoticed. One reason for this is that they are afraid of the unorthodox.

They confine themselves to the familiar highways of life. They know there are risks when you depart from the customary way. It is unfamiliar territory and it could lead to trouble.

They seldom dare.

Agreed: The travelled highway will get them to their destination quickly and safely, but the way is boring. Admittedly, it is the best way for busy people to travel, but they may miss the loveliness of a verdant valley, the sunshine radiant on the leaves and fields, the sight of ewes feeding their lambs beneath a spreading tree and the discovery of a sleepy village clotted about a frolicking stream where they can pause for a lunch that isn't standardized fare.

Should one depart the traveled road often? Of course not. But from time to time in life — dammit! — we need to break with the daily norms and do the unorthodox thing.

You can go on as you are, doing what is expected of you, logging your daily eight hours, following the accepted routines, refusing to take a chance, and probably end up being presented with the traditional gold watch. But be more enterprising, use your imagination, reject imposed limits, take a chance once in a while, and you may be the person *presenting* the watch.

Loosing the imagination

Imagination is a refusal to accept boundaries.

Not long ago, European maps had drawings depicting dragons at the limits of exploration. But there were men then who didn't believe in dragons, and they sailed courageously into the forbidding territory. They discovered not dragons but the Americas!

The successful have always been the people who reject boundaries, who challenge the accepted. They are the people who use their imagination, who are willing to shatter the mold, who will occasionally take a leap of faith.

I am not suggesting that you go off half-cocked, that you seek to be different for the sake of being different or that you mistake eccentricity for originality. What we are discussing here is the courage to loose one's imagination.

It is a law of life: The moment you stop growing you begin to die.

If we all did as our forebears did, the evolutionary process would end. Continue in business as you have always done and you will go bankrupt. The world will pass you by — it will be beating a path to the door of the guy who just invented a better mousetrap.

Imagination may be defined as forming a mental image of something not present in the senses. So, when you find yourself confronted by an apparently insoluble problem, study it. And when there seems to be no solution, loose your imagination.

William Zeckendorf, a colorful and enterprising real estate tycoon in the 1960s, prided himself on being a solver of problems. He exemplified the imaginative businessman, undaunted by obstacles and always ready to dare.

Born in Canada, he spent his latter years in New York City where even his going to work each morning was a production. His offices were the penthouse of the Chrysler Building, which he owned. Each day, he drove to Manhattan from his home in the country in a chauffeured limousine, license plate: ZECK-1. As he travelled, he kept his office alerted as to his exact whereabouts in traffic, established his schedule for the day and dictated to his secretary. The doorman at the Chrysler building was poised for his arrival. A private elevator was standing by to convey him at ear-popping speed to the top where his staff was lined up at the ready.

At a private luncheon he recounted to me how, at one point in his career, he decided to buy the entire city block of buildings between Macy's and Gimbel's, New York City's two largest department stores. He planned to refurbish the street-level area and lease it to the Woolworth company, so that when shoppers went from Macy's to Gimbel's they would pass through Woolworth's — surely good for business. Using proxies to hide his intentions, he bought the various properties needed. Only one obstacle remained: a decrepit fire hall in the middle of the block, which the city refused to sell him. It seemed the entire project would founder on this one rock.

Undeterred, he brought a piece of property nearby and built a modern fire hall, complete with sleeping quarters, a recreation hall, even showers for the firemen. He then offered it to the city for one dollar. They accepted it and Zeckendorf completed the deal for, as he described it, "the biggest damn Woolworth store in the world."

Confronting your fears

How can you break the string of cautious years and stir yourself to become the man or woman who is prepared to take a risk?

• The first step is to confront your fears.
• What are you afraid of?
• Why are you so hesitant to seize opportunities?

Is it because — to repeat the common excuses — you are doing very well where you are? Because you've been counseled since childhood to finish what you've begun? Because you don't want to take a chance of losing out? Because you'd rather leave well enough alone? Because you have responsibilities to others? Because you don't like to go out on a limb? Because you know the grass only looks greener on the other side? Or is it because there would be opposition at home?

These may be valid reasons for maintaining the status quo. But deep down is there not an awareness that you are cautious to a fault? Are you, in fact, going nowhere? Do you need to summon your courage and make a bid for a higher rung on the ladder? Don't thrust such thoughts away — nurture them.

Not failure but low aim is the mistake.

And don't postpone forever taking action while you debate with yourself whether or not to make a move, endlessly focusing on the problems rather than the possibilities.

I had lunch some years ago with Lester Pearson, Canada's Nobel Prize-winning Prime Minister, when he was reminiscing about American President Lyndon Johnson.

"I first met President Johnson at his ranch in Texas," Pearson said. "He had been in office only a few weeks. We were having serious problems on the Great Lakes at the time — rivalries within the Seafarers' Union, violence and shooting.

"I was told that Lyndon's aides were very nervous about our getting into matters of substance until the president had been better briefed. My people, too, were pressing me not to raise the Great Lakes question. Notes of caution were being raised on both sides.

We had no sooner sat down, both of us flanked by cadres of nervous advisers, when the president said, 'Look, Mike, let's you and me slip into the next room for a few minutes and let these guys get started.'

"The next room," Pearson said, "was a small sitting room. We pulled up comfortable chairs. Very relaxed. Very informal. Lyndon said, 'Mike, they tell me you're not very happy about certain union problems between our two countries. I don't know a hell of a lot about the problems, whatever they are, but the hell with that. Why don't we do this: You tell me what you want done that I can do without doing a disservice to the American people, and I'll see that it's done.'"

Pearson did. At seven the next morning, Johnson telephoned Paul Hall, head of the Seafarers' Union, and told him he was sending a car to pick him up and bring him to the White House for breakfast. There the problem was ironed out.

As Pearson finished the story, he threw his head back and laughed. "Sometimes," he said, "you don't pay attention to the Nervous Nellies."

We are all subject to the counsel of caution: "Careful now, don't go off the deep end." And we should be. But always to play it safe in life, never to stretch for the prize, never to go out on a limb, is to be a dull stick.

There is no avoiding risk in life. There is a fable about a man who, fearful of the risks of daily life, stocked his home with food and water and retired to empty rooms behind closed doors — only to trip over his beard and break his neck.

So, having decided to have done with undue hesitancy, act! Stop temporizing. Don't be the like the dog-lover who, faced with the need to dock his newborn puppy's tail could hardly bring himself to do it, and so cut off the puppy's tail an inch at a time.

U.S. General George Patton used to say to his officers: "Take calculated risks. That is quite different from being rash."

FOR REVIEW

(1) Too many of us play it safe. Sometimes you need to take a chance, to believe in yourself enough to go out on a limb. The very successful in business are those who challenge the norms. They are the people who use their imagination, the people who take calculated risks.

(2) Usually, we hesitate to take the leap of faith because we doubt ourselves. More often than not, this is because we are acutely aware of our own deficiencies.

(3) When you dare something unorthodox and succeed at it, it is seldom the result of luck. It is more likely to be the consequence of imaginative thought and careful planning.

(4) How can you break out of a tendency to be overcautious? The first step is to confront your fears. Ask yourself what you are afraid of? Why are you so hesitant to do the unorthodox thing?

(5) Don't postpone action forever while you debate with yourself endlessly examining the problems rather than the possibilities.

13 | Yes, You Too Can Be on Television

Television may be the single most important
invention of the twentieth century. It is certainly the most pervasive
and persuasive. There can be little doubt that it is the most powerful communications tool in history. Even a local cable outlet provides larger audiences than can be addressed through any other
medium.

Companies value and are prepared to pay for special skills, and
the ability "to come through the tube" is an invaluable skill. If you
want to succeed in business, you would be well advised to learn to
use television effectively.

The failure to do so could limit your drive for success.

You might dismiss television as unimportant in your career. "I'm
not a performer," you may say, "I'm a businessman. I may use television to advertise a product or a service, to promote the company
or to inform the public, but why should I trouble to learn how to
perform on it? The likelihood that I will ever use that ability is
remote."

This is a shortsighted and erroneous view.

Consider for a moment. Do you not regularly see business people appearing on television:

- In an interview?
- In an excerpt from a speech, on the news?
- On one of the increasing number of business programs?
- During a discussion of a community issue?
- Commenting on the economy or on trends in the society?
- Making a presentation at a convention?

Business-oriented television programs have proliferated in the past five years.

If you are successful at what you do, or if you have expertise in a particular field, you may be invited to make a guest appearance on television. If you have something to say and some facility at saying it, you may find yourself on frequent call. And beyond the personal satisfaction and the immediate benefits accruing from such appearances, there is a particular cachet that derives from being seen on the tiny screen.

A television appearance will give you an air of authority, a presumption of expertise — a valuable adjunct in a career.

Take the time to acquire the basic television skills, to develop them until you are at ease before the camera, and you may enhance your opportunities measurably.

It is not all that difficult to do.

Business men on television

You can get some sense of how effectively television can be used by looking at two men: Lee Iacocca, president of Chrysler Motor Company, and Victor Kiam, president of Remington Products. Iacocca has become a household name. His tough dynamism projects powerfully on the screen. Kiam, despite a less than prepossessing personality, is as well known as some television stars and is frequently asked for his autograph. And his highly personalized commercials have sold millions of electric shavers.

I am not, however, addressing myself here exclusively to senior executives. Most CEOs aren't, nor should they be, their company's public spokespersons. My comments are directed particularly to people in middle management and to those younger men and women whose careers are still in the embryo stage.

Your goal should be to develop an ability to use television effectively in the awareness that, having done so, opportunities to use the skill will present themselves in a number of ways:

- When there is a strike at the plant and someone is needed to explain management's side to the news media.
- When you are invited to participate in a closed-circuit discussion at a convention.
- When you must address the camera while preparing a presentation at a sales conference.
- When there is a new-product launch and someone is needed to make the presentation.
- When the company makes news and a television reporter comes around with a camera.
- When a local television crew comes to your office to record your views for the evening news.

There may be dozens of other opportunities. Oddly, however, most business people give little thought to television. As a consequence, they are ill at ease or inept on television and waste the opportunity.

This is a paradox, for most of them are leaders and should perform well on the tube. Most have an inner dynamism; it is one of the reasons for their success. They give thought to their physical appearance and to the impression they make. They are aware and alert. They know well that part of the success of any business is the face it presents to the public.

Nevertheless, most of them neglect to take the time needed to develop the ability to communicate through television.

Learning the basics

The first thing to learn about television is how it functions.

Things we don't understand tend to intimidate, and to most people an appearance on television is a frightening prospect. But, unless you are intending to become a specialist, all you need to know are the essentials. With the mystery gone, the experience will not be so intimidating and your first trip to the local TV station can be taken in stride.

Your introduction to the transmitting side of the medium will probably begin in the makeup room. Because of improvements in lighting and cameras, television makeup has become fairly complex. In earlier days, a virtually opaque pancake makeup was applied indiscriminately to cover the entire face and neck, "warts and all," but today's makeup artist works more carefully.

You will be directed to a small makeup room and seated in a modified barber's chair where a man or woman will apply a base and do extra work around the eyes and cheeks and chin. If you are balding, your forehead may be powdered to reduce the shine. Your hair may be toyed with. Play the rugged individualist, rejecting these ministrations, and you will be the loser. Under the studio lights without makeup, you may appear haggard. The shine on your brow will make you look sweaty and nervous. The circles under your eyes may deepen to bags.

You will then be directed to a studio (more often than not after interminable delays; television is like the army in its "Hurry up and wait" routines). TV studios are usually large, barnlike areas, gloomy places, with many lights "flown" from the high ceiling and with two or three cameras trailing cables across the floor. There will be a set, usually a news desk or a compact simulation of the corner of a living room or study.

If it is your first time behind the scenes, you will be surprised at how unimpressive, indeed how tacky everything seems.

Apart from the content of what you will say, there are only three things to be concerned with: your clothes, your demeanor and your posture.

Clothes: The rules are simple to the point of being nonexistent. Wear what you normally do. Avoid anything outlandish. If you are going to err, do it in the direction of informality — television is an informal medium. Unless the program is strictly business, avoid the three-piece suit: if you're wearing one, jettison the waistcoat. Plain colours are best but avoid bright red. Try not to wear any jazzy patterns or stripes.

The important fact to remember is that television is an intimate medium. Most of the time you will be seen on a medium close-up, so don't fuss and fret about your clothes.

Demeanor: Don't strain to make an impression; relax. Don't worry about whether your best side is to the camera — nothing is more transparent than self-conscious posing. If you normally talk with your hands, do so. Instruct yourself — insofar as you find it possible in an unnatural situation — to be yourself. That's what works on television; affectation and pompousness don't.

Be you — that's who they invited.

More important, that's what works.

Posture: There are few "don'ts" other than don't slump. In interview settings, the studio furniture tends to be of the nature of an easy chair or sofa, and most people settle in. Unfortunately, when you do, two things happen. A double chin or even the beginnings of one will be accentuated, and if you are more than a few pounds overweight the belly will bulge. On the other hand, don't sit ramrod straight; relax.

Apart from that, forget your posture and do what comes naturally.

The technical side of TV

There are two basic mechanisms in a telecast: the camera and the microphone.

To the uninitiated, the camera is a massive, robotic cyclops. Propelled by the cameraman, it glides silently around the floor and glares at you unblinkingly. It can be intimidating. There is no reason it should be, so disregard it.

The microphone is miniaturized and is no bigger than the first joint of your little finger. It will be attached to your clothing by a technician. There is little you can do about it, so forget it. One caveat: Don't touch or pound your chest. You may inadvertently strike the microphone, and the resultant boom will simulate a bomb blast.

The cameramen will have one objective: to transmit your visage to the home screen as clearly as possible. The sound man has a similar mission: to make your words perfectly audible. It is in their interest to do you justice. Trust the technicians to do their job; they are experts, and until you gain a great deal of experience, don't try to help.

The temptation to do so is great. We are all more or less vain. Before the camera you will tend to become self-conscious. Maybe you look better straight on than in profile, maybe your nose is a shade large or your eyes are too closely set or your Adam's apple too prominent. But there is nothing you can do about these faults at this point, so try to put them out of your mind.

More than that: Unless you were just named Miss America, you're not there because of your beauty.

Being yourself

Where should you look while the show is in progress? The rules are simple: Look at the interviewer when he or she is addressing you and, if you are one of a number of guests, at your fellow guests as they speak. Behave exactly as you would with a small group in a living room. The only things you ought not to look at are the camera and the ceiling.

You may be self-conscious about your voice. You may know that you tend to swallow the ends of sentences, that there is a slight sibilance on your S's and that there are certain consonants that give you trouble. Again, try to forget them. You are there because you have something to say that the producer feels is important, not because you are an elocutionist.

The activity around you will be less intimidating if you remember that everything is designed to assist you. Don't worry about the floor manager, the sound engineer, the lighting man and the camera men; unless you are a celebrity, they will be utterly indifferent to you. You are one of many strangers who come around each day, and then disappear.

Conversing with a camera

It is a different set of circumstances if you are being interviewed in what is termed a "remote" location — in your office, say, or out of doors — and the interviewer is not on camera. In this situation, speak directly to the camera lens. Don't stare at it fixedly, simply look at it as though it were a friend and speak as you would in conversation.

Because you are aware that what you are saying is being transmitted for miles around, you may think you should speak more loudly than normal. Don't. The effective tone in television is the conversational. Fix that fact in your mind.

I well recall my first venture into the medium. It was on the Columbia Broadcasting System national network from a studio in New York City. CBS, in cooperation with the National Council of Churches, had decided to commit a half-hour each Sunday morning to a series aimed at American youth and I was selected to be the host.

At the first rehearsal of the first show, I took a cue and began to talk to the camera. Almost immediately the director broke in on the studio intercom:

"Ten minutes, everybody. Charles, I'd like a word with you."

On the set he asked me, "How many people do you think will be listening to you?"

"I have no idea," I said. "The producer tells me three to five million."

He shook his head. "No."

"One million?"

"No."

"I give up," I said. "How many?"

"One."

"One? I don't understand."

"I was watching you from the booth a moment ago. Your voice was raised; you were talking to a crowd. But television is an intimate medium. You talk to individuals. Each person in the audience is listening to you in the privacy of the home, maybe dressed in a bathrobe or a T-shirt, maybe with a beer or a cup of coffee in hand.

You have to learn this: Nobody hears you as a crowd; each person hears you as an individual. The audience may be in the millions but" — he lowered his voice and emphasized the words — "Nobody hears as a crowd; each person hears as an individual.

"Talk to that one person just as you would if you were face to face."

It was the best advice a neophyte could have received.

So, when you are on camera, talk as if you were speaking to one person. In a very real sense the camera is one person — at the other end of the transmission is an individual sitting before a television set listening to you.

I learned to do it by visualizing a tiny gnome inside the camera and speaking directly, personally, to him. Others tell me they learned by talking to the person operating the camera. A network anchorman told me that he focuses on an imaginary blue spot just behind the lens and talks to it. It was said of a certain performer that she made love to the camera with her voice.

Learning by doing

How can you develop your skills in the field of television? How can you even begin to when you never get to appear?

By practice.

But how can you practice performing on television without going to a TV studio? In the same way you rehearsed public speaking: Find a private place and practice.

Use some object to act as a camera lens. It need be no more than a propped-up hand mirror, a clock, a table lamp. Place it at eye level anywhere from six to ten feet away and speak to it. But don't just maunder on; concentrate. Tell your "camera" about something that interests you. Try to convince some imaginary listener to accept what you're advocating.

Talk to him. Talk to her. Reach out toward that person until you can feel it. You'll be surprised how quickly a sense of intimacy will develop.

Your own "studio"

If you are determined to master the medium, you would be well advised to make an investment to that end. Buy your own "television" camera — a video camera. The great advantage is that you can study your performance, erase the tape and do it again.

The camera will also provide you with a unique record of your family's growth and development: birthdays and graduations, Christmases, fun in the garden or swimming pool. No other system for storing memories compares with it.

Apart from the challenge to become proficient in television broadcasting, why take the time and trouble?

It may be that you will decide to go into television as a vocation. This is not the place for a discussion of the medium as a career opportunity; the variety of jobs in the television industry is enormous, ranging from producer to director to on-camera "personality" to technician to set designer to writer to script-girl to time-salesperson to camera operator and on and on.

A word of caution: As one whose career in television has spanned some twenty-five years — as performer and producer — I would advise the person with stars in her eyes and dreams of fame and fortune in her thoughts to bear in mind that on-camera careers tend to be brief and are, more often than not, less than glamorous. Ten years before the camera is beyond the average, fifteen years is extraordinary and twenty years is exceedingly rare.

Nevertheless, television is the preeminent means of mass communication in our age, and it will be even more important in the future. And, if you learn how to communicate effectively on the TV screen, you may find that opportunities will arise in your company to act as a departmental or management spokesperson. Or to tape internal messages to staff. Or to narrate sales presentations.

There are any number of possibilities.

Prepare yourself for them.

FOR REVIEW

(1) Television is the most pervasive and persuasive invention of the twentieth century. Its outreach provides larger audiences than can be addressed through any other medium.

(2) There has been a proliferation of business-oriented television programs in recent years. Virtually every channel carries a business or investment program.

(3) Anyone intending to succeed in business should learn to use television effectively. Taking the time to acquire the basic television skills could enhance your career potential immeasurably.

(4) The individual who develops an ability to use television effectively will find numerous opportunities to use that skill.

(5) The single most important thing to be learned about performing on television is that you are being seen and heard by individuals rather than by an audience of thousands. Nobody hears as a crowd; each person hears as an individual. Talk to that person.

14 | Keeping Pace With a Changing World

THE MOST SIGNIFICANT NEW FACT in our time is the accelerating speed of change. Indifference to that fact is a guarantee of disaster. Disregard the changes taking place in our world and the future will simply pass you by.

Change is not new; it is of the essence of life. The only unchanging thing is change.

But you and I live in a period unlike any other in history. The speed of change is accelerating as never before. There have been more changes in the past one hundred years than in the previous ten thousand.

You can grasp how fundamental and how rapid these changes have been by realizing that, if a person who died at the turn of the century were to be resurrected and set down in a modern city, he would find our world almost unrecognizable.

At the the turn of the century there were no automobiles, no airplanes and few paved roads. There was no television. There were no computers, no skyscrapers, few elevators, no rapid transit, no motion pictures, no supermarkets, no electric refrigerators and no kitchen appliances. There were no communication satellites or space vehicles and no nuclear weapons. There was no Communist party.

(My wife adds: There were no pantyhose.)

And the pace of life has changed. A few decades ago, if you missed your train you would shrug and say, "That's okay. There'll be another one along tomorrow." Today, if you go downtown shopping and miss the first section of a revolving door, you feel behind schedule for the remainder of the day.

As the song says: "The world she is a-changin'."

Our values have changed

At the turn of the century the church and the synagogue determined the moral and ethical standards of society. On a sabbath morning, dressed in their finest, people went to church or synagogue and spent the remainder of the day in restricted activity. Places of business were closed. Places of amusement were dark. Even sports events were restricted. Rigid censorship of books, magazines and films was observed. You didn't trouble to lock your doors when you left the house; lawbreaking was rare. Divorce was uncommon and the participants in it were shunned socially. Modesty was the norm: a glimpse of a woman's ankle was arousing and even men wore tops on their bathing suits.

Today, the established religions have little influence on society. Services are sparsely attended, and the membership is graying. Millions of men and women live together "without benefit of clergy." Sunday is increasingly a day of commerce. Movie theaters are jammed. Sports fans throng parks and stadia. Nudity and hard-core pornography are a commonplace. Drugs are available everywhere.

Our family relationships have changed

At the turn of the century, the father was the undisputed head of the house and his word was law. The home was a patriarchy. A man's wife and children did as they were told. Children were to be seen and not heard. If in the unlikely circumstance that there was a serious marital dispute and an appeal was made to the courts, the man would be sustained. A wife and children were a man's property, and they had few rights. Women didn't even have the vote. Divorce was rare, but in those instances where it was granted, the wife had no legal claim on the estate.

Our social attitudes have changed

At the turn of the century no respectable young woman was permitted to spend time in the company of a young man without a third party present — the ubiquitous chaperone. No woman smoked. There was little sexual intimacy until the late teens. Even engaged couples were seldom left alone in situations that might appear compromising. If a young man was able to borrow his father's horse and buggy to take a young lady of his acquaintance for a ride, they could travel only short distances. And if they managed to find a secluded spot on the outskirts of town where they wouldn't be recognized, someone would probably recognize the horse.

Today, in his automobile, a young man and his date can be miles from home and shacked up under a pseudonym in a motel within an hour.

Our sense of neighborhood has changed

At the turn of the century people belonged to a community. They knew their neighbors and shared life with them. As children grew to adulthood, they married within the neighborhood, settled there and sent their children to the schools they had attended.

Today a majority of young people can't wait to get away from home. More often than not they scorn their parents' values. The public school no longer regards it as within its mandate to teach value systems, and there is little sense of community. Many families live in high-rises and condominiums and don't even know the names of the people who live beside, above or beneath them, separated from them by only a wall, a ceiling or a floor.

Nor, in most cases, do they want to.

At the turn of the century, business was done on the basis of a handshake; a man's word was his bond. Today it is *caveat emptor:* let the buyer beware.

At the turn of the century our lives were governed by tradition. Today, the fact that a practice is traditional is itself a good reason for challenging it.

As a consequence of these and other changes, we no longer know what to think about relations:

- Between the sexes.
- Between parents and children.
- Between neighbors in a community.
- Between citizens and their government.

Change and the world of business

I draw attention to these changes not to moralize or to rue the loss of a simpler day — it is pointless to curse the clock — but to make the point that, just as the speed of change in our century makes the nineteenth century seem like a snail's pace, the acceleration of the speed of change in the tomorrows will make today's frenetic pace seem like dawdling.

Recognition of this fact is profoundly important to anyone in business, whether that person is a chief executive officer, a senior manager, a buyer, an entrepreneur, the vendor of a product or a service, a truck driver or a file clerk.

Changes in society effect changes in business, and changes in business affect society. Not only the dramatic technological changes, such as computer networking or robotics, but the subtler changes in attitudes and values. All have had a profound effect on the marketplace and on the men and women who toil in it.

In a world where a fully automated assembly line can replace five hundred people with five, where a computer can accomplish Herculean inventory and bookkeeping tasks and where imports can outmode and underprice anything locally produced, the man or woman who fails to give serious thought to the effects of change on business and on individuals is courting disaster.

Adapt or perish

The multitude of inventions and the improvements in techniques that have become a part of our daily living in recent decades are transforming our world. And with that transformation accelerating daily, everyone in business, at whatever level, must ask these three questions:

- Am I keeping pace with these changes?
- Is the field I am in threatened by these changes?
- Is the company I work for in danger of becoming outmoded?

A company or an individual who fails to keep abreast of the changes in our society and in the world is in danger of ending up a commercial castaway.

The basic law of life is this: Adapt or perish.

For millions of years, as the environment of our planet changed or other factors intervened, any creature that failed to adapt became extinct. But as some creatures disappeared, others found the changes propitious and prospered. The situation is the same with man; it is for us as it is for every other creature: Adapt to change or perish.

This is true not only in the general sense but also in the particular. Just as nuclear explosives and our indifference to the pollution of the environment threaten our extinction, so the changes effected by technology and competition jeopardize our way of life.

Let it be stated baldly: *The company and the individual who do not have the foresight, the wisdom and the drive to keep abreast of the changes now taking place in the marketplace will perish.*

Where are these changes of which we speak most evidently at work? In technology, in the marketplace and in the worker.

The introduction of a new technology can revolutionize a society swiftly and profoundly. I recall as vividly as if it were last week standing in uncontained eagerness outside a small automobile showroom on Yonge Street in north Toronto when I was a boy.

I was one of a crowd so large that it spilled into the street and disrupted the traffic. We were gathered for the public introduction of the first Model A Ford car. Henry Ford, who had already sold fifteen million duplicates of his Model T, had said of the Model A: "You can have it in any color you like so long as it's black."

Came the climactic moment of the revelation. To heighten our anticipation, the windows of the showroom had been covered with wide strips of butcher paper. Suddenly, and somewhat untidily, the salesmen began to tear away the paper strips, and there, revealed in all its modest glory, was the Model A — the first Ford with a gearshift!

The crowd emitted an audible sigh. We were on the edge of a new age.

Primitive as they now appear, those early automobiles were the beginning of a revolution. They fundamentally changed our society. It is almost impossible to measure their impact.

A world changed by commerce

An automobile requires steel, so mines were sunk and rolling mills were built. It demands gasoline, so people fanned out across the world, drilling into the earth's crust, and the oil business was created. It requires rubber, so trees were tapped and ships were built to transport the rubber from around the world. It needs smooth passage, so muddy lanes became streets and streets became roads and highways, arteries of commerce that changed the landscape and carried goods and people everywhere and made the nation a neighborhood.

The automobile evolved. Gigantic tractor-trailers reduced the once mighty railroads to secondary status. Buses virtually ended passenger travel by train. The automobile created the mobile generation and the dormitory community. It shrank distances; it ended isolation; it created ghost towns and built great cities and effected countless other changes.

Significantly, by outmoding horses, it put tens of thousands of men and women out of work even as it created jobs for many more.

It altered our world.

You can grasp how profoundly the automobile has changed our society if you travel to a third-world country. You can see exemplified there a way of life little changed for centuries.

Today, other inventions, some as revolutionary as the automobile, are about to alter our society further.

A notable example is communication.

For millions of years, the transmission of a thought from one person's mind to another's required that they be face to face. The invention of electricity changed that. Soon the wireless made it possible to send messages across continents and around the globe in seconds. Radio enabled us to communicate simultaneously with millions of our fellows. Television added the visual aspect.

When, in 1969, astronaut Neil Armstrong set foot on the moon's surface and spoke the memorable words, "One small step for a man; one giant step for mankind," some two hundred million people watched him and heard his words even as he spoke them.

Electricity increasingly works its wonders. A bank of computers can do the work of a thousand mathematicians. The instantaneous transmission of printed data annihilates distances. Robots make gangs of toiling workers redundant.

And, as Al Jolson said, "You ain't seen nuthin' yet."

The shrinking world of business

The question becomes: Are you, is your company, staying abreast of such changes?

Among them, the movement of the geographical center of business.

At the beginning of the century, the center of world commerce was in Europe. Between the world wars, the center shifted to the Atlantic rim. After 1945 it localized in the United States. Today, with the emergence of Japan and other Asian countries, it has moved to the Pacific rim.

You need not go to the Orient to grasp the mushrooming commercial growth of the area. You can see images of urban Japan on the television news. Tokyo is as affluent as any city in the world. The summer Olympics showed Seoul to be one of the world's most modern cities. Hong Kong is a mini-Manhattan. High-rises and modern buildings contour the skyline in dozens of Far Eastern cities.

The emergence of east Asia as a commercial and financial center is the single most important fact in today's business. You need only to examine the shelves in a department store or watch the passing automobiles to see how pervasive that influence is.

But the Far Eastern intrusion into the Western way of life should be seen as a challenge, as a galvanizing rather than an intimidating fact. What many North Americans overlook in the commercial flowering of the Orient is the fact that Asians are not simply potential competition: they are potential customers.

As Mark McCormack notes in his book, *What They Don't Teach You at Harvard Business School*, "You can count on your fingers the American companies which are maximizing their full potential in international markets." Then, with the born salesman's ability to sense a prospect, he adds, "There are eight billion people out there [in the world] and fewer than three percent of that eight billion live in the United States."

The relatively few businesspeople who do contemplate the potential Asian market have learned that the Far East is no longer that far away.

The Far East on your doorstep

Beyond the potential market for North American products in Asia, few in business have realized that immigrants are increasingly a part of the consumer market at home. The international world of commerce is not "out there"; it is on your doorstep.

The flow of Asian immigrants to the Western world, and particularly to North America, is one of the most significant phenomena of our time. Walk the streets of any major Canadian or American city and you will see the distinctive faces of Asiatics, Indians and Pakistanis. Nor are they all "struggling immigrants"; you will glimpse them passing by in luxury automobiles and shopping in the upscale stores.

Scan the daily newspaper and you will read that the Japanese and other Easterners are building branch plants in North America, taking over prestigious businesses, buying downtown high-rises (it is estimated that Asians own forty percent of the high-rises in the Los Angeles area) and purchasing many of the most desirable homes in the great cities.

I was in Toronto's magnificent Eaton Centre recently, and with my wife went to look for a dress for her mother, a petite woman. To our surprise, there was a large department specializing in clothes for smaller women. A salesclerk told me the department had been expanded recently to cater to the increasing number of Asiatic women frequenting the store, many of whom are smaller than their Western counterparts.

In Toronto there are 300,000 Italians, 135,000 Europeans, 126,000 Chinese and approximately the same number of Portuguese and newcomers from the Indian subcontinent.

Immigrants — they are an increasing part of today's and tomorrow's consumer market. But how many businesses take pains to appeal to them? Are they a focus of attention or even a passing thought when most companies draft their marketing plans?

The challenge of tomorrow

But there is a far greater challenge to business, a more fundamental one: The economic dominance of the West is being challenged.

World trade is in the beginning days of a transition unparalleled in history. As one respected economic expert has said, "The center of world economic gravity is shifting rapidly toward Asia and the Pacific."

Many business people are, of course, aware of the fundamental and swiftly accelerating changes taking place, but a majority have not yet begun to understand how profound these changes are and how widespread the ramifications will be.

The influx of foreign goods has been well noted — how could it not be? Japanese steel, machine tools, automobiles, motorcycles, television sets and other electrical goods have become dominant. We have not been able to compete in either quality or price and have been driven out of the market. This has been dismissed by some as an aberration, a problem of consequence but not a dislocation, but surely anyone with a sense of perspective can see in this the early evidence of a decline in the economic dominance of the United States.

These new and accelerating shifts in global productivity seem likely to alter our future radically. They will almost certainly bring about the destruction of some businesses and the weakening of others as the revolution in trade continues and gives rise to super-corporations and global conglomerates larger than anything we have yet imagined.

The dimensions of change

One can glimpse how massive the coming changes will be by looking closely at the economic growth in the Pacific region in recent years.

It is commonly assumed that the threat to Western commercial dominance comes primarily from that economic powerhouse, Japan. But this conclusion overlooks the rapidly changing giant, the People's Republic of China, not to mention the newly industrializing countries, Taiwan, South Korea, Hong Kong and Singapore, and the established industrial states of Australia and New Zealand.

All these Pacific region countries have in recent years had a rate of economic expansion that has far eclipsed those of the traditional western powers.

In 1960, the combined domestic product of the Asian-Pacific countries was a mere 7.8 percent of the world's total. By 1982 that figure had more than doubled. Since then the area's growth rates have exceeded those of Europe, the United States and the USSR by increasingly wider margins. By the year 2000, the Pacific region countries will probably produce more than twenty percent of the world's gross domestic product — the equal of Europe and the United States.

The surprise in the Far East has been the remarkably swift economic expansion of the People's Republic of China. One in five of the world's people live there. If its astonishing industrial growth can be sustained, it promises to transform that enormous country within a few decades and make it a formidable competitor in world markets.

The new European challenge

But the threat to Western economic and industrial dominance does not come only from the Pacific region. Less noted has been the emerging potential of that other awakening giant, the European Economic Community.

With the adherence of Spain and Portugal, the EEC's twelve-nation population now totals around 320 million: fifty million more than the USSR and almost half as big again as the United States. The total gross national product of the EEC is close to that of the USA and its share of world GNP is far larger than Japan, the Soviet Union or China. Although there are great disparities in average income between its member states, the EEC is much wealthier than the whole of the USSR, and some of its members (West Germany in particular) are richer per capita than the United States. Despite the fact that the consortium faces many problems of consequence, it is clearly signaling a renewed and major competitor in world trade.

Add to this this the likelihood that Gorbachev's Russia will become a major factor on the world stage as a competitor and a customer, and the challenge from Europe becomes even more significant.

But despite these and other imminent changes in the world of commerce, not many Western businesspeople are factoring them into their plans. How we will deal with tomorrow's opportunities — and its risks — is the fundamental question of our time. To fail to address it is to be like the driver who careers at undiminished speed down a highway clearly marked with danger signals.

It is, of course, impossible within the brief compass of this chapter to deal specifically with how the opportunities and the problems of the future may be met. My purpose here been to raise an alert. Enough to say that the challenge is also an opportunity and to emphasize that it will be impossible to succeed in business — however one may try — unless there is an acute awareness of the fundamental changes happening in the world of commerce and steps are taken to keep abreast of the swiftly changing patterns of trade.

To be indifferent to these changes and to fail to consider them in one's corporate and personal planning is to invite calamity.

An anonymous scribe in another century said: "Times change and we change with them."

He might have added, "Or else!"

FOR REVIEW

(1) The most significant new fact in our time is the accelerating speed of change. There have been more changes in the past one hundred years than in the previous ten thousand. Disregard this and the future will simply pass you by.

(2) The changes in our way of life are fundamental: Our values have changed. Our social attitudes have changed. Our family relationships have changed. Our sense of neighborhood has changed. The entire world of business has changed.

(3) The man or woman in business must ask these questions: Am I personally keeping pace with these changes? Are my particular skills threatened by these changes? Is the company I work for in danger of becoming outmoded?

(4) The emergence of Pacific Asia and other areas as commercial and financial centers is the most important new fact in today's business. Not to act on this knowledge is to court disaster.

(5) What many individuals and businesses forget is that the emerging nations are not simply competitors, they are potential customers.

Business Books for Successful Managers

PIATKUS BUSINESS BOOKS have been created for people like you, busy executives and managers who need expert knowledge readily available in a clear and easy-to-follow format. All the books are written by specialists in their field. They will help you improve your skills quickly and effortlessly in the workplace and on a personal level.

Each book is packed with ideas and good advice which can be put into practice immediately. Titles include:

The Best Person for the Job Malcolm Bird

The Complete Time Management System Christian H. Godefroy and John Clark

How to Collect the Money You are Owed Malcolm Bird

How to Develop and Profit from Your Creative Powers Michael LeBoeuf

How to Win Customers and Keep Them for Life Michael LeBoeuf

Leadership Skills for Every Manager Jim Clemmer and Art McNeil

Powerspeak: The Complete Guide to Public Speaking and Communication Dorothy Leeds

Smart Questions for Successful Managers Dorothy Leeds

The Strategy of Meetings George David Kieffer

Your Memory Kenneth L. Higbee

You too can benefit from expert advice. Just look out for our distinctive Piatkus silver business book jackets in the shops. For a free brochure with further information on our complete range of business titles, please write to:

Business Books Department
Piatkus Books
5 Windmill Street
London, W1P 1HF

PIATKUS

LEADERSHIP SKILLS FOR EVERY MANAGER
by Jim Clemmer and Art McNeil

Here is a book which offers managers new techniques to improv
organisational effectiveness. It shows how, by developing leadershi
skills throughout a company, the right ideas can be transformed int
profitable, bottom line results. With practical examples, highlighte
discussions, charts and quotations, managers, executives and supei
visors will find *Leadership Skills for Every Manager* an invaluabl
catalyst for effective action.

Jim Clemmer and Art McNeil are founders and operating execu
tives of The Achieve Group, a Canadian company dedicated to help
ing organisations improve quality, customer service, innovation an
productivity.

THE STRATEGY OF MEETINGS
by George David Kieffer

Meetings are central to business and professional life. They are where
you reach decisions, make deals and manage people, and they give
you prime opportunities to boost your own career. Using a wide
range of strategies, lawyer and businessman George David Kieffei
shows you how you can make any meeting work for you.

'Kieffer shows how meetings are central to your own career success
and effective management. His book will change forever the way you
conduct yourself in meetings.' – *Kenneth Blanchard PhD, co-authoi
of 'The One-Minute Manager'*

'His book is must reading for anyone who participates in meetings,
from novice to chairman of the board.' – *Harold M. Williams, president and Chief Executive Officer of the J. Paul Getty Trust*

'. . . full of sound conventional advice, as relevant to schools anc
colleges as to corporations . . .' – *The Times Educational Supplemeni*

SMART QUESTIONS FOR SUCCESSFUL MANAGERS
by Dorothy Leeds

The first book on a new strategy for getting ahead, *Smart Questions for Successful Managers* is addressed to managers at every level, from trainees to managing directors. Using anecdotes, case histories and lists of possible questions, it is designed to:

- Test your overall questioning approach
- Assess your ability for getting the most from your staff
- Evaluate the way you use questions to advance your career
- Help you to become a more effective manager

Offering a technique to help you become a more effective manager, it covers such topics as: training, problem solving, negotiating, getting a rise, delegating and interviewing. In today's business world, the managers who succeed are not necessarily those who think they have all the right answers: it's asking the right questions at the right time that leads to success.

Dorothy Leeds runs a management consultancy firm in the United States. She is a specialist in communication skills.

HOW TO COLLECT THE MONEY YOU ARE OWED
by Malcolm Bird

Getting paid on time is vital for any business. In *How to Collect the Money You are Owed*, Malcolm Bird gives practical advice on how to organise your invoicing and money collecting systems, improve your cash flow and increase your profitability.

- Learn how to control your cash flow cycle
- Develop an efficient invoicing system
- Get to know your clients and how they operate
- Learn how to chase up money effectively
- Discover what to do if all else fails

How to Collect the Money You are Owed will help you save time and money. It is an essential handbook for every office.

Malcolm Bird is the Development Director of an international insurance company.